The
Restorer's Handbook
of
Drawings and Prints

Under the direction of Madeleine Hours, chief curator of the National Museums of France, Master of Research at the National Center for Scientific Research.

The
Restorer's Handbook
of
Drawings and Prints

Robert Lepeltier

 VAN NOSTRAND REINHOLD COMPANY

New York   Cincinnati   Toronto   London   Melbourne

English translation: Anne G. Ward

Copyright © 1977 by Office du Livre, Fribourg (Switzerland)

Library of Congress Catalog Card Number: 77-5591

ISBN 0-442-24765-6

Printed in Switzerland

Published in 1977 by Van Nostrand Reinhold Company
A division of Litton Educational Publishing, Inc.
450 West 33rd Street, New York, NY 10001, U.S.A.

Van Nostrand Reinhold Limited
1410 Birchmount Road, Scarborough, Ontario MIP 2E7, Canada

Van Nostrand Reinhold Australia Pty. Ltd.
17 Queen Street, Mitcham, Victoria 3132, Australia

Van Nostrand Reinhold Company Limited
Molly Millars Lane, Wokingham, Berkshire, England

16 15 14 13 12 11 10 9 8 7 6 5 4 3 2 1

Library of Congress Cataloging in Publication Data

Lepeltier, Robert.

The restorer's handbook of drawings and prints.

Translation of Restauration des dessins et estampes.

Bibliography: p. 123

Includes index.

1. Drawing – Conservation and restoration. 2. Prints – Conservation and restoration. I. Title.

NC930.L4613   760.028   77-5591

ISBN 0-442-24765-6

TABLE OF CONTENTS

Acknowledgments

I should like to express my gratitude to the curators of the Bibliothèque Nationale, the Archives de France, the Musée Carnavalet, the Fondation Custodia (Dutch Institute) and the Musée de Rouen, who have all been most helpful while this work was in progress.

The technicians in the various departmental workshops of the Bibliothèque Nationale have shared their skills with exemplary kindness, and the same scholarly and helpful collaboration has been extended to me by my junior colleagues Monique Duchâteau, Dominique Taralon and Dominique Le Marois. Our discussions, even when we disagreed, supplied the basis of this book.

The unfailing assistance of the Laboratoire de Recherche des Musées de France, and especially that of Mme Lola Faillant, who drew up the bibliography, has been invaluable.

I must also thank my son Pierre, who is a connoisseur of art, for the help he has given with the editing and illustration of the book.

Finally, I owe a debt of gratitude to the memory of my father, who was my finest teacher.

8

INTRODUCTION

COLLECTION

The making of images is one of the earliest signs of civilization, and the clearest and most evocative expression of the human spirit. Man made the image, took pleasure in it, and preserved it with care. As time passed he tirelessly continued to leave his marks on a wide variety of materials, experimenting for the purposes of his art with some of the hardest substances such as stone or metal and some of the most flexible such as paper or skin.

Whatever the message they may convey, be it sacred or simply the expression of an aesthetic feeling, the works of mankind are meant to last. This is not surprising, since in man the need to preserve is allied to the survival instinct. He knows that he is destined to die, and consoles himself by remembering that his images will live on after him.

The Ancient World

There is no evidence that engraved stone or metal was ever treated with any particular care, but the ancient world furnishes numerous indications of the ceaseless vigilance with which works inscribed on fragile materials were constantly surrounded. The Egyptians, Greeks and Romans all had libraries. Like us, they had to find ingenious solutions to the problems of humidity and desiccation and infestation by insects.

Manuscripts were kept rolled up inside wooden or ivory cylinders, and bundles were packed in bindings of the same material. Papyri and parchments were treated to protect them from insects and mildew, though it is doubtful whether the vegetable agents used for this purpose, such as camphor and eucalyptus, were ever very effective.

The ancient traditions were continued in the Middle Ages and, although no rules of conservation or restoration were ever formulated, great care was taken of the fine illuminated parchments created in many cultural centres. The great beauty of the bindings testifies to the fact that preservation was a matter of importance.

The Beginnings of Graphic Art

The invention of paper soon raised the whole question afresh. Its appearance five hundred years ago marked the real birth of graphic art in the western world. Men shortly came to prefer this light, vulnerable, inflammable, soluble and easily creased material as a medium for self-expression, and covered paper with superficial lines and fugitive colours. It was extraordinary that such a frail material should be chosen for such a destiny.

A new medium always has some obvious advantages. Despite its apparent fragility it is sturdy. It can be produced in quantity; it adapts easily to the requirements of art and writing.

In the era known as the Renaissance writers, artists and craftsmen were immediately attracted by this new expressive medium. It cannot have been mere coincidence that printing was invented at roughly the same time as paper. A great flowering of processes, techniques, styles and crafts swiftly arose and flourished from this combination, and this gave rise to the spread of graphic art in the west. Within a few decades the output of works of art on paper became immense. From the fifteenth century onwards prints and drawings on paper reached

1
◄ Frontispiece: Drawing in red chalk framed under glass (François Boucher).

10

perfection, produced masters and gained a public following.

The First Collectors

The history of collecting these works begins at this time. Two-colour portrait drawings enjoyed great popularity in the courts of Europe. Catherine de' Medici's collection was an outstanding example.

In Italy the writer, painter and architect Giorgio Vasari (1511–74) assembled a vast work in several volumes entitled *Libro dei Disegni*, which strikingly reflects the era's passion for the acquisition and preservation of drawings on paper.

Before long the number of collections had increased, and some distinguished collectors' names were bracketed with the work of the great masters. Thus is justice done to patrons who were not always kind to the artists but devotedly preserved their works.

CONSERVATION AND RESTORATION

Scientific restoration and classification is a very recent idea – it barely goes back fifty years – but it must be admitted that the vast bulk of graphic art which has accumulated over the course of five hundred years and is now kept in museums, libraries and private collections could never have survived without the constant care and enlightened attention bestowed on prints and drawings long before the modern age.

The great collectors originally received the drawings from the artist or dealer in the form of simple sheets of paper. They made their selection, and then entrusted them to craftsmen or pupils who lined them or made an ornamental mount according to current well-documented methods. These mounts strengthened the drawings and made them a uniform size so that they could be gathered together in sets or portfolios. Small drawings were grouped on the blank pages of albums. The use of glazing to protect drawings is a much more recent development. As to prints, their natural place was in books which were well protected by their bindings.

These early methods of collecting and assembling were surely the best safeguard for works of graphic art. Exceptions to these rules were inevitably destined to perish. They ended up pinned to studio walls or blown away by the wind.

The Decline in Conservation Conditions

Conditions necessary for the survival of works executed on paper have deteriorated progressively right down to the present day.

At first the great collections were handed down as a whole from one person of high rank to another. Noblemen passed them on to bankers who in turn gave them to royalty. Later they changed hands more frequently and haphazardly, and the great collections gradually broke up.

The establishment and development of an 'art market' made no small contribution to this trend. From the eighteenth century onwards public sales became more frequent. Collections of prints and drawings were subjected to public auctions, and to bartering or even liquidation in the hands of collectors who, though progressively more numerous and widespread, were often disastrously ill-informed.

Deterioration of Materials

All this time artists were steadily growing more indifferent to the quality and durability of their tools and paper. These were no longer made in the artists' studios, with the pupils grinding the colours and cutting the black and red chalk from the block; artists now bought their supplies from 'colour merchants'. Furthermore, the craft of paper-making by hand, a real art in itself, was abandoned in favour of mechanical processes which produced commonplace, vulgar-looking paper. More and more supplementary material and chemical agents were added to the paste instead of rags, which were becoming rare; wood, which is less rich and fine in quality, was used.

From this time onwards great and minor masters executed their works on mediocre paper with pencils and colours of dubious composition.

The Increasing Numbers of Works of Art

Works in ever-increasing numbers were added to the artistic heritage already accumulated by preceding generations. Minor works were now included and helped to augment the natural trend.

It became steadily easier to count as 'art' works of less importance, unfinished pieces and engravings which were no more than trial pieces. Works that earlier artists had regarded as intermediate stages or preliminary sketches, drafts, notes from nature, copies for later use or trial pieces were carefully collected and treasured.

The development of new printing processes such as lithography and improved woodcuts sparked off an explosion in the art form and changed it into a very common means of reproduction. The invention of photography did nothing to halt this chain reaction. This fantastic proliferation did not necessarily make the conditions of works on paper any worse, but it certainly made the search for reasonable methods of conservation more urgent.

Methodical Conservation and Scientific Restoration

Fortunately the revolutionary era of the eighteenth century witnessed the beginning, and the nineteenth the expansion, of a general widespread concern for the preservation of works of art. The conservation of public property became one of the duties of the state.

Taking over from the great collectors, museums were established to house the former royal collections which were pouring in from all sides, often in considerable disorder. The foundation of the public collections – which, incidentally, checked the rate of expansion of private collections for only a short time – played a decisive part in ensuring the survival of works executed on paper and postponed the inevitable demise of works threatened by age. Advances in the study of the history of art, techniques and science made it possible to approach the problems of conservation and restoration scientifically. Chaptal, Vauquelin, Brongniart and Chevreul in France and Davy and Faraday in England were studying the structure of paper and colours, the influence of environment and deterioration due to animal and vegetable factors.

Scientific advances led to the production of better paper, pencils, colours and inks of high quality, and also adhesives, solvents and bleaches suitable for artists and restorers. With them came apparatus for disinfecting, laminating and analysing paper by means of which great numbers of works could now be saved.

All the time, these discoveries were being published and made widely available in international journals. Emigration and exchange visits by qualified experts as well as the frequent movement of the works themselves combined to accelerate an awakening of conscience and a feeling of general responsibility towards them.

The Function of Modern Restoration

Nowadays scientific knowledge and apparatus seem to have reached a peak. The part played by restoration in the maintenance of the arts, including graphic work, is recognized by collectors, dealers, museumn curators and public authorities alike. Alongside this general growth of a sense of responsibility, a universal demand for restorers, official, independent or amateur, has arisen. Nevertheless, there are still a great many different approaches to the purpose and method of restoration.

The dealer is looking for someone to remove stains and foxing which may lower the price of the work.

The collector's perpetual problem is a drawing which has been damaged in packing.

The museum curator, that watchful guardian of public property, entrusts damaged masterpieces to the restorer to keep them in the best possible condition.

Sometimes the faded portrait of an ancestor or a drawing of a vanished scene has to be restored.

And finally, impressive collections are left by artists, great masters and simple amateurs, which must be preserved from oblivion or destruction.

Unfortunately it is not usually the real well-being of the work which interests its guardians, but only superficially visible damage. Whether it is undertaken for the sake of commercial value, or keeping our artistic heritage intact, or preserving a gift of sentimental value, restoration is not only expected to arrest the visible processes of deterioration but also to eliminate every trace of it.

As well as owners who entrust pieces to the most orthodox restorers, there are others who abandon them to inevitable destruction by their neglect or reluctance to subject them to interference which they regard as sacrilege, but there are plenty more who hand them over for deliberate 'improvement' or even complete renovation, much to the detriment of the artist's original conception.

Almost the same thing could be said in the same words of faked working-over, uninformed or clumsy interference, and mistaken refraining from action or salvage operations.

Restoration: A Part of Preservation

In practice, restoration is only justified when it is regarded as a natural component of the task of conservation.

Works of art have a very fragile constitution which is determined by the artist. The pencil line on paper, the distribution of colour and tone – in a word everything the artist uses to express his conception – is irreplaceable and ought to be inviolate.

Unfortunately, they all age. Deterioration of paper and fading lines and colours are not shameful misfortunes that befall some prints and drawings while others are lucky enough to escape altogether; they are the common lot of graphic works executed on a perishable support with fugitive lines. The attentive care of curators and collectors can only slow down and postpone their inevitable dissolution.

Working with them the restorer must be constantly on the watch in order to determine the best environment and time for action. Since he has formed an accurate idea of the conditions for the preservation of both public and private collections, he can suggest the appropriate measures to ensure the survival of the works and to avoid accidents which might damage them. Being aware of the mischief caused by excessive dryness or humidity he can easily show how fine drawings can fade away in the corner of a drawing room, over a radiator, in a shaft of sunlight, or on a wall saturated with damp. He can slow down or arrest the attacks of parasites and the development of mildew.

Among the advantages of restoration are the protective measures which the restorer, always more awake than others to the causes of degeneration, is in a position to suggest in order to provide the best preventatives. Surprisingly enough, alongside the great state collections, privately endowed restoration institutes and the enlightened amateurs assisted by skilled restorers; there are still many equally important collections, some public, others the entire contents of studios, in untrained hands with no access to experts in preventative measures and the correct treatment of works of art.

Prints and drawings, which may have been intended for museums, are thus abandoned to well-meaning amateurs devoid of direction or control, and to haphazard restorers who treat them according to their own personal fads and fancies.

A Plea for Generally Accepted Principles

It is time for everyone with works of art in their care, be they administrators of public or private collections, dealers, official or amateur restorers, craftsmen, framers and mounters or anyone who is responsible in one capacity or another for handling or dealing with works of art to get together to define generally acceptable principles, compare notes, make known the effect of new techniques, pinpoint the best methods, and introduce them to the public at large. Before it can reach maturity, the science of restoration must emerge from the shadows and acquire laws and a philosophy rooted in art history and universal recognition of its importance to the survival of our artistic heritage.

This book does not aim to be a course in restoration and it does not set out indisputable principles and unalterable formulae. It is rather an introduction to the techniques of restoration, an invitation to ponder on the principles which should guide every restorer, and perhaps also a chance to initiate a debate, sincere but unprejudiced, open to everybody, technical but without scientific prejudgments, devoted entirely to the subject of the salvation of the treasures of graphic art.

ANALYSIS OF WORKS OF ART

Examination and Analysis of Graphic Works

Before restoration begins a graphic work is carefully examined in every detail. This examination enables the restorer to make a diagnosis before deciding on a course of treatment and plan of procedure. An art historian, expert or amateur will use the same basic analytic techniques, but the restorer has to combine their differing approaches with his own specialist knowledge and experience.

Before he can make an accurate diagnosis and work out the best plan of procedure the restorer needs to acquire detailed information about the work's material composition, the condition of its various components and how they will react to the envisaged treatment. This means that he must go beyond a straightforward study of the work's external appearance: the print or drawing nearly always has to be unmounted and the analysis continues throughout the course of the restoration.

The above remarks are sufficient to show that it is not a restorer's job to apply a treatment prescribed by a third party; at each stage of the restoration he carries complete responsibility for both diagnosis and result.

2

Drawing in black chalk, stump, printed and highlighted with pastel on the verso. The drawing has a rectangular frame with an oval panel and is split vertically from top to bottom (John Downman, *Portrait of a Lady*).

VISUAL EXAMINATION

This provides a basis for the material, historical and aesthetic analyses.

All the materials that make up the mount and support are examined to determine their nature, age, present condition and to detect possible previous restoration. First the picture is examined under a good light, recto and verso, then on a light table and, if necessary, with the aid of optical instruments such as a lens or weaver's glass.

All the materials used in the execution of the work are carefully scrutinized. The restorer will have no trouble in recognizing different graphic techniques or identifying the kind of pencil or tool used, the type of ink and its binding agent, the composition of the colours and their probable degree of stability.

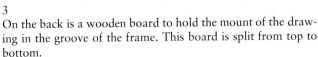

3
On the back is a wooden board to hold the mount of the drawing in the groove of the frame. This board is split from top to bottom.

4
Photograph in raking light. This shows the drawing after it was removed from its frame and makes the causes of deterioration obvious: the sheet is rectangular in shape and has been stuck on all four sides to a cardboard support. The difference in the coefficients of expansion of paper and cardboard explains the horizontal split and the wrinkles in the sheet.

An aesthetic and stylistic analysis follows to complete and reinforce the conclusions of the initial investigation. It is often very useful – indeed indispensable for works of great value and interest – to prepare a file at this point to hold the information resulting from the examination. It will include photographic evidence of the original condition of the work and a description of the restorations accomplished. The restorer must be careful not to miss any clue in this investigation, for example, a handwritten or printed label, a seal, signature or collector's, mounter's or saleroom stamp.

PHYSICAL EXAMINATION

If a more searching investigation seems necessary, the restorer can have recourse to some of the

17

5
A photograph of this drawing taken in normal light, after unframing, emphasizes a horizontal split (already noted on the preceding illustration) and the damage caused by exposure to light which has turned the paper in the oval panel brown. The lighter patches were caused by spots on the glass which formed a screen.

6
The same portrait photographed in infra-red light produces a print which shows the drawing in all its original freshness. The brown oval and the marks disappear completely in this type of light, which suggests that the damage is superficial.

7
The drawing has been removed from its cardboard support by soaking. In view of the fragility of the paper, it was immediately strengthened with a backing stretched over the old paper and

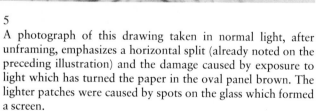

immersed in bleaching baths as soon as it had been backed, ▶ although backing is usually done after bleaching. It was then placed in a press to dry.

18

techniques already commonly employed for paintings (cf. *Conservation and Scientific Analysis of Painting* by Madeleine Hours).

Photography and radiography can be used to underline and confirm the visual diagnosis or bring to light tell-tale signs that were invisible to the eye. The restorer should have all the available techniques at his disposal: raking light, micro and macro-photography, X-ray photography, etc. (Figs. 2–7). The considerable research and interpretative work that has been undertaken so successfully in the field of paintings gives a glimpse of the possibilities offered by the scientific analysis of graphic art.

CHEMICAL EXAMINATION

Information produced by chemical analysis can make an equally vital contribution to a correct diagnosis. There are several different tests, some quite simple, that provide these data.

The size used is analysed to determine its nature and strength. To do this solvents (principally water, acetone or alcohol) are applied to a limited and marginal area of the work.

The paper's acidity is measured by means of a pH meter or by the use of indicators.

The solubility and fugacity of the inks and colours is tested *in situ* or on a cut-off section using solvents, a bleach or by immersion.

Although these tests must be conducted with discretion it is vital that nothing is left out, for their purpose is to provide an assurance that the materials involved will withstand the treatment envisaged for the restoration.

The restorer will take into account the results of these various examinations when he makes his decision whether or not to restore, but he must give equal weight to other considerations that may seem to have nothing to do with the work of art itself. An estimation of the work's value (historic, artistic or monetary), while not influencing the diagnosis, will affect the choice and extent of the treatment. In making his decision the restorer has to bear in mind that alternatives exist and that it is always best to opt for whichever treatment is the simplest, longest-lasting, most reliable, most easily reversed and, often, the cheapest. If a sophisticated and complicated venture risks damaging the work of art, then it is best abandoned.

The descriptions that follow will perhaps leave the reader with the impression that to prescribe and carry out a restorative treatment is a simple matter. This would be a mistake. The restorer must be bold in tackling his work, but he must also approach it calmly and soberly. We have often had to spend several months of reflection before launching into a risky undertaking and for particularly difficult cases to solicit the advice of colleagues. Nevertheless, after analysis, reflection and consultation a satisfactory means can usually be found to repair damages to a graphic work.

Finally the work must be got under way, and the materials and practical methods organized – important factors for success. Later we shall describe the restorer's workshop, equipment and materials in greater detail. We may comment on their complexity or simplicity or seem to prefer craftsmanship to results obtained by extensively equipped institutions, but we wish to close this section by stating quite clearly that the quality of a restoration depends ultimately on the knowledge, intelligence and skill of whoever carries it out.

Survey of Components and Techniques

Graphic art is characterized by the effect of a certain kind of printing or drawing technique on a certain kind of support. Consequently, anything that affects the support or the strokes and colours will damage the quality of this partnership.

THE SUPPORT

The very best support for graphic works nowadays is, without doubt, paper in all its various forms. Paper is, however, a complex and relatively recent material. At one time artists used more primitive substances some of which, after periods in and out of favour, continue in use today.

Paper

Both history and legend place the origin of paper in China at the beginning of the second century A.D. With commercial trading and successive waves of migrants, it crossed Asia, reached the Mediterranean, got to Italy and Spain and finally arrived in France in the fourteenth century and in England in the sixteenth. At the end of the sixteenth century it was taken to America by seafarers, and it did not appear in Philadelphia until the last years of the following century.

During all this time paper was hand-made with the aid of simple tools and rudimentary machinery. The eighteenth century brought a growing and increasingly exacting demand for paper, which the old techniques and crude materials were quite incapable of satisfying. The paper industry was born.

But despite the technical and manufacturing developments and the variations in quality, the basic principle of the composition of paper remains the binding together of cellulose fibres to form a mesh to which will be added size and various other substances. The cellulose fibres suspended in water (paper pulp) are spread on to a porous stone slab to drain. The sheet thus formed is pressed, dried, sized, treated or calendered.

– *Cellulose fibres* are obtained by the mechanical or chemical break-down of rags, vegetable fibres, wood, etc. These fibres are what give the paper its strength.

– *Particles of kaolin,* talc, calcium carbonate, etc. are added to the fibres to give weight, whence their name, 'loadings'. The loadings help lower the cost of the paper, but they are not a desirable ingredient. They abound in poor quality paper, debasing it and encouraging decomposition. Conversely, very fibrous papers (rag-paper, security paper, mulberry paper, etc.) are remarkably resilient.

– *Size* (animal, vegetable or synthetic) binds together the cellulose fibres, holds the loadings and gives the material body. Size is also responsible for the paper's smooth finish, renders it resistant to writing inks and allows colour to be successfully applied. The absence of size (blotting paper or engraving paper) results in a porous and often weak paper.

The relative proportions of these three components (to which colorants, additives and dressings can be added if and when required) and the manufacturing processes used are open to infinite variation and can produce as many different types of paper.

The most common of these can be classified in the following groups:

- newsprint (posters, collages)
- writing and printing paper (most prints and drawings)
- cardboard and wrapping paper (mounts and frames)
- speciality paper, treated or dressed (laminated paper, tracing paper, wax paper, glassine, corrugated paper, etc.).

To which can be added the old-fashioned hand-made paper (from rags) and paper from the Far East (made from vegetable fibres).

Early Supports
Before paper came on the scene man engraved, scratched, painted and dyed simple materials from the mineral kingdom (hard, soft or precious stones), the animal kingdom (bone, ivory, shells, leather, parchment and vellum) or the vegetable kingdom (wood, bark, papyrus). Very few of these different materials, with the exception of parchment, vellum and papyrus, resemble paper in texture, components or appearance; and each requires a special restoration technique.

Manufactured and Composite Supports
Artificial, manufactured or reconstituted materials form the last category in the range of graphic supports; namely metal, glass, ceramic and fabric. These products existed long before the advent of paper, but although nowadays they may occasionally compete with it, they are unable to replace it. Graphics that come closest in nature to painted canvasses are those executed on light-weight tightly woven fabrics (silk, taffeta) or on looser weaves that have been sized or dressed. Into this category come some of the Far Eastern wash-tints, silk-prints or drawings and some pastel drawings. These composite materials deteriorate in a way analogous to that of paper, and the techniques of restoration are related.

Modern Synthetic Supports
Synthetic film, fabric and other materials are often similar to paper in appearance and can often be used in a similar way. They are, nevertheless, restored according to entirely different principles.

GRAPHIC TECHNIQUES
The impression made on the support can coincide with the creative act to produce the original work of art, or it can come after it, in which case it is called a reproduction. Some works fall between the two, retouched or tinted engravings, for example, or stencil prints and serigraphs. There is a noticeable difference in the appearance of the strokes, the degree to which they penetrate the support, and also in the effect of the colours, depending on whether the printing process is carried out mechanically or by hand.

Hand Processes
The impression of the tool and the colour it applies merge to form the stroke.

– *The impression:* Some tools leave an impression only; they engrave the support (a stylus on wax, a

8
Original red chalk drawing (Antoine Watteau, *Three Soldiers*).

burin or etcher's needle on metal). Most leave a line or stroke of colour (metal point on coated paper, natural stones, chalk, red chalk, carbon black, reconstituted minerals or crayons, Fig. 8).
The picture's resistance to deleterious factors (scuffing, desiccation, damp) will increase the deep-

er the support is incised and the more vigorously the pigment is applied.

– *Solid colours:* Some materials, in particular charcoal, chalk, crayon and a very soft tool such as a stump, leave a mark that is so superficial that the

least rubbing will erase it. The only way of preserving it is the use of a varnish or binding agent to fix it to the surface of the paper.

– *Liquid colours:* Ink, wash, watercolour and gouache are all solutions or emulsions of colour pigments and are applied by brush, pen or spray. The extent to which the liquid penetrates the paper depends on the consistency of the solution. The pigment is concentrated on the surface, diffusing slightly through the support. Ink, wash or watercolour will usually penetrate deeper than gouache which remains more on the surface. The tool (brush, stylus, bamboo stalk) sometimes leaves its own impression along the strokes of colour. By their nature and also because they soak deep into the fabric of the paper, liquid colours are particularly resistant to superficial and mechanical damage. On the other hand they are extremely vulnerable to even a slight degree of humidity which makes them run or dissolves them.

Mechanical Processes
An original work of art can be reproduced, but a reproduction cannot itself be considered a work of art unless it is printed directly from the artist's original work: his woodblock or engraved metal, his design on a lithographic stone, or stencils prepared by him.
There can be one, unique reproduction (the counter-proof or monotype) or a limited edition (printed

9
Detail of an engraving (×25) showing the imprint of the oily ink in the paper (Jean Lepautre).

24

from his engraving). The creative process is in two stages, and photographic or industrial reproductions are not included in this category.

Most of these processes involve transferring colour pigments from a support on to paper by means of uniform mechanical pressure. A double is faithfully produced, a copy of the artist's work but without his individual touch.

Engravings

The restorer is more concerned with the engraver's choice of inks and paper than with his techniques. Whether the printing method be intaglio or relief, on a wood, metal or stone block, the ink used is generally a pigment bound by an oily substance (linseed oil, glycerine, Fig. 9), with the exception of Japanese prints for which sized pigments are used. The ink is deposited on the paper more superficially in relief engravings than with intaglio where it is accompanied by the imprint of the matrix. But even if the ink penetrates the paper only slightly, its binding agent is a powerful fixative of colour pigments.

The paper chosen is generally fibrous and low in size, to facilitate the impression.

Other Methods of Reproduction

Reproduction techniques are numerous and open to infinite variation. As well as the great classic processes there are stencils, serigraphs, lino and woodcuts, blind stamps, counter-proofs, transfers and monotypes. What matters above all to the restorer is the nature and fugacity of the strokes and colours, how deeply they have penetrated the paper, the quality of the latter and the relationship between the two.

Deterioration of Prints and Drawings

ENVIRONMENT

A graphic work begins to age almost before it is finished, and the environment into which it is placed can modify or accelerate the process. Acting in isolation or together; humidity, temperature, light and air bring about the slow, natural, physical and chemical deterioration of paper, strokes and colours.

In this section we are going to specify the best conditions for the conservation of drawings and engravings. Works kept in less favourable surroundings can be expected to sustain some degree of damage.

Humidity

Paper is a hygroscopic substance: it has a natural tendency to absorb water from the atmosphere, a quality that enables it to maintain its coherence, suppleness and flexibility. In rooms that house drawings and engravings the level of humidity in the air must be strictly controlled.

Humidity is measured in terms of 'relative humidity'. The relative humidity, or R.H., of a given volume of air is the relation between the quantity h of humidity actually contained in that same volume and the quantity H necessary to attain the saturation point at the same temperature:

$$R.H. = (h/H \times 100)\%$$

The apparatus used to measure R.H. are called hygrometers and psychrometers. The optimum degree of relative humidity is between 45 and 55 per cent at a temperature of 20 °C/68 °F.

Excessive or insufficient humidity can be corrected by the use of air conditioners, humidifiers or dehumidifiers, which will effectively re-establish suitable atmospheric conditions.

Insufficient Humidity

A too-dry atmosphere, less than 40 per cent R.H., will make paper stiff and brittle. Prolonged exposure to such conditions could destroy it. If the desiccation is not too advanced the paper will become supple again when moved into a satisfactory atmosphere. If permanently and seriously damaged it will disintegrate and will have to be reinforced with patches or a lining. Newsprint and tracing paper are particularly susceptible to dessication.

Excessive Humidity

Too great a degree of humidity will dissolve the size in the support and in the mount and boards. This will weaken and eventually destroy the paper. The first remedy to try is simply transferring the work to a normal atmosphere; then, if there is a significant loss of size, re-sizing or lining the paper. It is almost impossible to restore strokes that have been weakened and colours that have become diffused because of moisture absorption or excessive humidity in the air.

As it softens paper expands. The extent to which it does so varies depending on the type and format of the paper and the degree of humidity in the air. Thus mounts, linings and patches composed of different types of paper or board react in different ways to a rise in relative humidity. The result is crinkles, bulges and cockles which are even more pronounced if the damp is unevenly spread.

To reduce the damage the lined or mounted picture can be moved to an atmosphere of normal humidity. If the trouble persists and does not respond to pressing, the whole structure will have to be unmounted (mount, lining or patching) and put together again after each separate part has been allowed to dry out. Excessive humidity encourages the propagation of vegetable and biological germs that proliferate in the air (Fig. 11). By a process called hydrolysis it also brings about chemical reactions between the paper's constituents and some of the gasses present in the air. The resulting degradation, although not strictly caused by humidity, is activated by it.

Light

While light is obviously necessary for the contemplation of prints and drawings, it is nonetheless an active and insidious enemy. Both natural and artificial light give out radiation that is dangerous to paper, notably ultra-violet and infra-red rays. The photochemical action of these rays on various substances and impurities in paper (lignin, acids, resins, etc.) results in a break-down of the cellulose fibres, which causes the colours to become bleached or yellow. Many inks and colours fade in the light and strokes are weakened.

For these reasons it is a grave mistake to expose graphic works – and in particular drawings – to light radiation unless they are being exhibited for a specific purpose, in other words, to be examined or admired. Exposure must be of limited duration, and the light intensity carefully checked, a control easily carried out by means of a light meter. The average

10
Watercolour with gouache. Considerable damage has been caused by exposure to humidity (Jonny Audy).

acceptable level that is both comfortable for the eye and safe for the drawing is 150 lux. A work of art can be kept in this light intensity without great danger. There are various ways to protect graphic works from damage caused by light. To start with, it should not be deemed necessary to put them on permanent display; the accepted practice should be to keep them carefully stored in folios or in specially designed accommodation. Positive measures (other than controlling the light intensity) can be taken to protect works dedicated to exhibition: sunlight can

be intercepted at windows and doors by the use of blinds, screens or filters and even by little curtains covering the works themselves. Filters can also be used to neutralize artificial light sources. The length of time for exhibition remains a matter for the keeper's discretion, but it should be a great deal shorter than is generally supposed.

Overexposure

A graphic work takes on a patina as a result of the paper browning under the light. This is for the most part unavoidable but in some cases it is disastrous. Sheets of drawings or prints exposed irregularly or partially to the light (border hidden by a frame, spots or cloudiness on the glass forming a screen, book page left open) retain the marks of the exposure on the uncovered zones. The patches show up lighter or sometimes darker depending on the kind of paper and its original colour. Discrete bleaching can reduce the contrast but these unpleasant-looking blemishes are hard to remove.

Underexposure

Another danger lurks at the other extreme. The absence of light, linked with other factors (humidity, inadequate ventilation, etc.), creates conditions in which micro-organisms, insects and rodents can develop and thrive.

11
Pencil drawing highlighted with gouache on beige paper. The spots are caused by humidity. They have been eradicated in the lower part by the localized use of chloramine (Anonymous, nineteenth century).

Air

Air contributes in two ways to the degenerative process in paper: as a vehicle for dust, spores, bacteria, etc. and through the action of its chemical components. There is no absolute protection against atmospheric pollution. For collections that are particularly threatened, filtering and air-conditioning are prescribed. In general terms the best advice would be to avoid siting a collection in an obviously polluted area (near a road, industrial installations or domestic heating apparatus) and to protect it from air-borne menaces by keeping it stored in suitable cases, cabinets and folios. The noxious effect of the air is reinforced by excessive humidity and accelerated by a high temperature.

Some elements in the air, such as carbon monoxide, nitrogen, ozone and sulphur dioxide, change the constituents of paper by hydrolysis, oxidation or catalysis. Sulphur dioxide, in particular, is catalysed by impurities in paper and transformed into sulphuric acid which destroys cellulose fibres. The paper becomes brittle and then disintegrates. Restoration in a case like this involves deacidification and then backing of some kind.

Hydrogen sulphide in the air transforms the lead carbonate in white gouache and pastel colours into black lead sulphide, completely altering the appearance of a picture. To correct this the blackened strokes or colours can be treated with a solution of hydrogen peroxide.

Oxygen may efface drawings produced with tin stone (used by J.-B. Carpeaux among others) as it transforms tin into white tin oxide. A possible regenerative treatment would be the sulphuration of the white stannic oxide into sepia brown stannous sulphide.

The air is a vehicle for spores and bacteria which settle on paper and wait until conditions are favourable for their development.

It also carries greasy or tarry dust, ashes and other mineral and vegetable particles which lodge in the pores of the paper and darken its surface, forming often immovable stains. The effects of the dust are reduced by brushing and possibly by gentle rubbing with an eraser. A bath of pure water with a trace of soap will deal with most stains. The salt contained in sea air fixes moisture on to paper, and so any work threatened in this way must be carefully insulated.

Temperature

A temperature agreeable to people, that is 20 °C/68 °F is also highly recommendable for the conservation of graphic works. About ten degrees above or below this level is also tolerable, but abnormal temperature conditions appreciably hasten ageing in paper. It has been calculated that a sheet of paper kept in a temperature of 100 °C/212 °F for 72 hours presents the same signs of ageing as paper kept in a normal temperature for 25 years. Temperature alone, except in extreme conditions (burning heat or intense cold), has only a mildly damaging effect on prints and drawings. It becomes particularly dangerous, however, when associated with other factors. It sets off chemical reactions which damage cellulose fibres and encourages the development of micro-organisms and the growth of mould. Finally, as we have already seen, temperature and humidity are complementary factors. The quantity of water effectively found in air at a given rate of humidity is all the greater the higher the temperature. This means that a rise in temperature increases the deleterious effects of moisture absorbed into paper. A high temperature together with a moist atmosphere is found particularly in tropical countries, but excessive heat conditions can also exist in apartments and houses, near heating apparatus, fireplaces or electric lights in showcases or windows that receive sunlight. A normal temperature can be regained by regulating the heating, ventilation and air-conditioning.

BIOLOGICAL AGENTS

Paper is the favourite food of all kinds of parasites, and they leave ample evidence of their existence.

Vegetation and Bacteria

Several hundred different varieties of spore and bacteria live in the air. Heat (above 25 °C/77 °F) and humidity (R.H. above 70 per cent) encourage their proliferation. In badly ventilated places they thrive just as well in the shade as in the light. They attack paper and feed on size, proteins, loadings, metallic salts and any impurities. Paper weak in pH and very hygroscopic paper are particularly vulnerable while close-woven or calendered paper has greater resistance.

At first the presence of this vegetation and bacteria

12
Drawing in bistre ink which has corroded the paper in places. Impregnation with moisture released a ring-mark caused by the ink spreading (Jacob de Gheyn).

13
Various incorrect patches on the back which will have to be removed to allow complete lining.

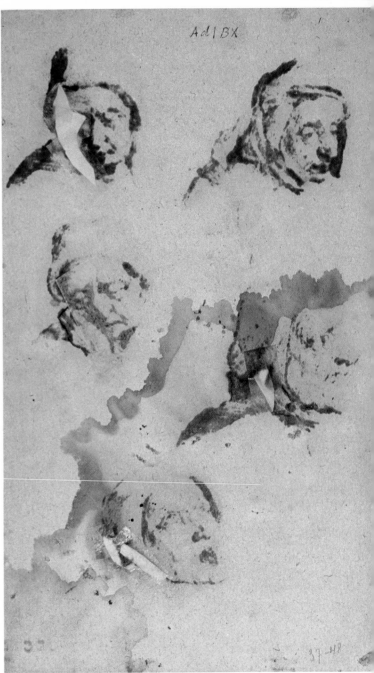

14
An example of the damage that an insect can cause in the mount is shown when the layers are separated.

is not easy to discern. Then they begin to appear as isolated and unobtrusive yellowy spots which spread out into brown, red, black and bluish patches, depending on the type of parasite. If the picture receives no attention they eventually join up to form a furry layer. Parasites attack all the components of paper, breaking down the cellulose fibres and rendering the paper weak and liable to tear. Then they penetrate into the layers of pastel and gouache and destroy inks, strokes and colours. They invade nearby material, cardboard, wood, fabric, leather, even plastic. An invasion of parasites can completely ruin a work of art and its mount, and this ultimate condition is irremediable.

The extent of the damage depends on how long it is before the presence of parasites is discovered. The picture should immediately be disinfected by vaporization, fumigation, spraying or soaking, in a vacuum chamber or airtight box. It is a good idea to disinfect before any symptoms appear, especially if other restorations are in progress (sizing or liquid treatment) or if the conservation areas are undergoing general sanitization. A dusting or brushing is often sufficient to get rid of surface contamination. Spots caused by parasite damage – foxing, freckling, mould – can be reduced by local or general bleaching. The treatment for major attacks accompanied by a weakening of the size or break-down of cellulose fibres is to re-size or possibly line the paper. Multiple or extensive lacunae are usually irregular in shape and sometimes (as seldom as possible) need to have their damaged edges levelled off before being filled in.

Insects

Of the insects that attack paper the best-known are silverfish, cockroaches and termites (Fig. 14). They work their way into mounts, bindings and even frames, feeding on size, paper, leather, fabric, wood and leaving holes, stains, deposits, droppings, eggs and larvae behind. Flies will dirty an unprotected work by depositing their excrement on it. Attacks of this kind indicate negligent conservation and faulty surveillance of the areas where the works of art are kept.

The damaged picture should first be removed from the infested place and then sterilized, disinfected and disinsectized using the techniques described elsewhere. Only then can the various deposits be scraped off and an attempt be made to erase the stains. If they persist the paper or just the discoloured areas should be bleached. Paper pulp can be used to fill worm-holes and small perforations. If the perforations are numerous and have attacked a delicate type of paper the print or drawing will have to be lined. It is worth adding that the restored work should be put back into a place that has itself been cleansed.

Rodents

Rats, mice and other rodents will automatically attack pictures whether they are scattered about, piled up or stored away, and mutilate the paper, fabric and wood. They do not feed on these materials but they can inflict fairly extensive damage. A small species such as mice leave droppings which soil the paper. Rodents are difficult pests to control because poison impregnated into the paper seems to have no effect. A full-scale campaign has to be launched with traps and bait containing ratkiller or repellants. In some extreme cases the only way to protect works of art from rodents is to keep them in metal containers.

Small amputations can be patched. Big ones are irremediable.

Other animals

All animals, particularly domestic ones, should be kept away if one wishes to prevent paper being accidentally marked by paws, claws, beaks and excrement. Stains will usually give way to bleaching. Tears and holes can be patched. Scratches can be reduced if the paper is dampened and then pressed.

MAN

The principal and indomitable enemy of all works of art – and by far the most destructive – remains man himself. He is responsible in one way or another for the conditions in which paper is kept and cared for. He is the villain behind every crime committed on works of art, either directly or by allowing the damage to be done.

Serious Damage

A great many graphic works have disappeared through war, riots, vandalism, migrations, transportations, theft and fires. The extent of these losses is unimaginable. Works that escape are usually seriously and irremediably damaged. Sheets are found with great tears, gaping holes, sections missing and varying degrees of burns; there are prints and drawings from which the strokes have been effaced and the inks and colours diluted and which at best have lost their original purity and freshness.

Large tears: Drawings that have been extensively lacerated or cut in two or more pieces have to be completely re-lined. The edges of the tears should be joined together as neatly as possible, although a permanent scar cannot be avoided (Fig. 17).
Perforations, holes, missing fragments: Holes caused by bullets, broken glass and battering can be repaired by patching or, if they are very big, lining. Extensively damaged works can only be abandoned.

Burns: Holes caused by burning and scorching have reddish-brown edges, and there is an irregular darkening of the entire picture surface, caused by the flames and fumes. Before applying patches the restorer can eliminate these marks by bleaching or by carefully trimming as little as possible of the affected areas (Fig. 18).

Miscellaneous marks: Water and mud leave various kinds of stains and marks on graphic works: spots, halos, bulges, cockles, accompanied occasionally by a partial break-down of cellulose tissues. Pictures collected together in boxes, piled up in cabinets and chests, or simply framed, risk becoming stained as a result of absorbing moisture from the materials touching them. They need to be completely un-mounted, dried and pressed. Then the stains can be removed and, if necessary, the paper strengthened by re-sizing. There is, with rare exceptions, no remedy when strokes, inks and pigments become diluted and lose their brilliance.

Minor Damage

Pictures rarely survive extensive damage, and it is often a miracle if they do. Most of the prints and drawings (even those in large private or public collections) that come into the restorer's hands have been marred by little accidents caused by negligence or carelessness, minor deteriorations that spoil their freshness and integrity.

15
There is a gaping hole in this print but none of the paper is missing (Japanese print).

16
The edges of the tear are drawn together, then the print is lined with mulberry paper to hold it in position. It is replaced in its mount, which was not damaged.

34

18
A burn in the middle of a print. The scorched edges will have to be removed before a patch can be applied.

19/20
A burn calls for extensive cutting. The edges of the burn have ▶ been clipped off to match the dark surrounding in the composition. The print has been lined. A patch has filled the gap; the colours have been restored with watercolours (lithograph by Fernand Léger).

17
A traced design extensively torn, creased and perforated by bad handling.

Folds and creases: Paper that has been accidentally creased for any length of time will be marked with wrinkles which show up in the light. Creasing encourages tears by damaging the fibres, and it breaks up non-liquid materials such as chalk and gouache (Fig. 21).

Any light folds can be pressed out, but as creasing renders the paper susceptible to tears it is better dealt with by relining (Fig. 22). In all but serious cases (Fig. 23) the paper can be made perfectly smooth again, and any damaged lines and strokes can be restored.

Tears, cuts and knocks: Prints and drawings are repeatedly being handled, carried about and referred to, and so they are constantly suffering damage (Figs. 26 and 27). Corners of loose leaves are particularly vulnerable; they crease and then break. Tears appear along the edges, at first slight and few in number but then getting steadily worse. Prints kept loose in cartons are rapidly defaced by knocks, tugs and scuffings, and the same applies to badly protected drawings. Small tears and cuts can be corrected by applying a small amount of paste to the lips and drawing them together, possibly reinforcing them with small pieces of paper.

Missing corners can be made good by sticking a narrow strip of paper of a similar kind to the back of the picture. The marks left by knocks and scuffings can be pressed out.

Various kinds of stain: Together with tears the most common accidents are stains caused by touching, rubbing, absorption or splashing. Some marks are only superficial (charcoal, pencil, ash, etc.), others have sunk into the paper (ink, grease [Fig. 28], coloured liquids of all kinds, etc.), and others again change the look and structure of the paper (acids, alkalines, etc.).

Marks that come into the first category can be eliminated by brushing and rubbing with an eraser. Stains of liquid origin can be reduced by the solvents and bleaching agents, listed in the Technical Notes. Such a treatment can be applied locally or the work can be completely immersed (Fig. 59). If damage is done to the appearance and structure of paper by corrosive liquids, the process cannot be reversed, although its effects can be lessened by some kind of reinforcement of the sheet (filling with paper pulp, re-sizing, patching or lining).

Pictures in immaculate condition are rare. Graphic works, with their fragile and somewhat ephemeral support, cannot escape minor blemishes, although attentive conservation and care will do much to avoid them. When all else fails creases, tears, stains, effacements and all the various forms of deterioration that prints and drawings undergo should be rapidly restored. Each time a work is damaged it becomes weaker and even more vulnerable to attack. Creases encourage tears, tears get bigger, whole pieces come off and are lost. Stains and effacements spread and get worse. The natural ageing process of all the materials is speeded up so that, if care is not taken, the print or drawing will soon be in a state of ruin.

There can be no doubt at all that it is better to conserve than to restore. There comes a time, however, during the inevitable ageing process of a drawing, when restoration is appropriate, indeed indispensable, even at the cost of some slight violation of the work's purity and integrity. For example, the timely lining of fragile paper (tracing paper, posters)

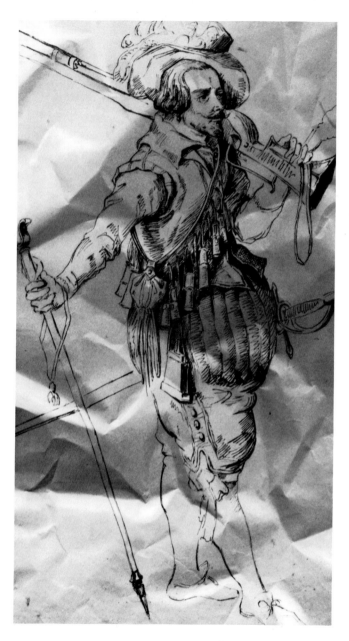

21
Pen-and-ink drawing. The creases could be completely removed by putting it in a press (Anonymous, nineteenth century).

22
A hole in the middle of a print caused by folding in two directions.

23
A crease in a drawing lined immediately before its execution. A mark like this, made before the drawing was executed, cannot be eradicated (François Verdier, *Assumption of the Virgin).*

could halt or limit its degeneration, and fixing charcoal and pastels will do the same for strokes and colours. The restorer must use his insight to choose the right time for these operations, and he should be fully aware of both the inconveniences and the risks of abstaining.

Bad Habits in Conservation and Mounting

Graphic works that have been mounted and are well cared for are still not infallibly safe from deterioration. Even in the artist's studio the drawn or engraved sheet is in peril. The artist himself is often a mediocre conserver: he pins his work on the wall, cuts it up, sticks sketches haphazardly on to boxes and then, at best, stores them away loose in cartons (Figs. 29 and 30).

In the most famous collections and even in museums (in spite of great precautions) pictures become marked, worn and sometimes torn and stained while being referred to, displayed or moved about.

But more serious still are the deplorable habits of some neophyte collectors, framers and art-lovers who – through ignorance, negligence or simply arrogance – annotate, cut up, stick down and otherwise abuse works of art.

Superfluous inscriptions: Any original or very old annotations should be respected, especially any with a historical character such as signatures, of course, and attributions, captions, dates, initials and collector's stamps. On the other hand the restorer would be justified in erasing, scraping off or dissolving pencil or ink annotations that bear no relation to the work or are of nno interest.

Collectors are strongly advised to confine any remark, attribution or reference to the mount or, if there is no alternative, to the back of the picture.

Scuffings or effacings: Graphic works that are inadequately mounted and badly stored (squashed or piled up, stacked face to face, rolled or folded) will get rubbed and scuffed, the strokes and colours will transfer, and the pictures will become blurred and muddy (Fig. 31).

The only remedy for this is the careful, methodical use of an eraser, but the picture's original clean, sharp appearance will never be recaptured.

24
The whole paper bears the marks of excessive folding (poster by Robert Delaunay).

25
The restorer lines it with strong paper so as to smooth it and remove all traces of folds.

Incorrect use of glues and adhesives: Some adhesives should be banned from the amateur's, mounter's or framer's arsenal (Fig. 32). Glues used for mounting prints and drawings should be water-soluble and colourless pastes.
Any marks left by unsuitable or impure glues (sour paste, cellulose glue, etc.) or adhesives (sealing wafers, self-adhesive tape) can be eliminated by their solvents.

Removing pictures from their mounts and albums: Exceptional works that have been part of great col-

43

lections are usually mounted. A mount supports and protects a picture, but it is also a valuable token of the work's historical destiny and as such should be preserved. To be avoided at all costs is the incompetent amateur's practice of tearing apart mounts, albums and bindings in order to isolate a single drawing or transfer a picture to a modern mount (Fig. 33).

Unfortunately old mounts sometimes come apart and are detached from the drawing. Indeed restorative work itself usually involves unmounting the

26/27
Pencil drawing (Amedeo Modigliani, *Portrait of a Man*). The badly crumpled and torn paper has been lined and the gaps filled in.

28
A large patch of old oil on a print has hardened the paper and ▶ caused obstinate wrinkles.

picture. Whenever possible equal pains should be taken with the mount as with the drawing, and it is important to disinfect and deacidify it at this stage. Both mount and drawing should be put together again after the restoration is complete.

Incompetent Restoration

The cure is sometimes worse than the illness. Woe to any work of art that falls into the hands of an imprudent restorer, an inexperienced or arrogant amateur, an ignorant or clumsy framer who indiscriminately wields paste, bleach, pencil and brush!

Mishandling that affects the paper's structure: Paper will weaken and its surface become rough if an eraser is too vigorously applied, or if it is excessively scratched or brushed, or if it is subjected to a prolonged bath in bleach, solvents or even pure water. It will show signs of peeling and flaws, breaks and holes will appear. Sheets thus maltreated will have to be sized or lined.

Incorrect tension: Any pasting and gluing job should be carried out with due regard both to the principles of paper expansion and to the properties of the materials used (glue, paper, board). Clumsy lining, mounting and framing applies too much or too little tension to the print or drawing. Fragile paper, notably window-mounted tracing paper, will split if overstretched. Linings will cockle if not properly stretched or pressed. In either case the whole structure will have to be taken apart and done again according to the rules.

Use of wrong materials: Besides being unaesthetic, bad quality paper and board are frequently the

29
A print which has been stored loose in a cardboard box has been damaged all round the edges.

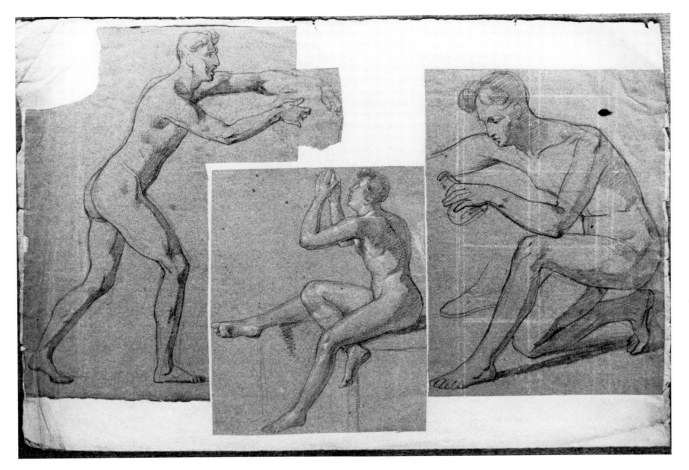

30
Several studio sketches mounted as a group, probably by the artist himself.

root-cause of degeneration in prints and drawings, and this factor should be rigorously checked. The quality of a support is not judged solely in terms of appearance: it has to be related to scientifically decreed standards of sterility, inertia, acidity and 'permanence/durability'. The same goes for all the materials used – glues, colours, chemical products, solutions, pencils and tools. They should be of the highest quality and properly adapted for their appointed task. Innovations and heresies are dangerous and to be avoided. Engravings mounted between two sheets of glass or plastic become damp in the confined space and victims of condensation. Sheets of drawings stuck to wood or strained on canvas will become distorted and absorb foreign substances which will stain and deface them. If he is

31
This pencil drawing was kept for a long time unmounted and in contact with others, and as a result, was completely covered with traces of graphite. Only large areas with no lines on them have been treated with an eraser, so that the picture is partially cleaned (Alexandre Théophile Steinlen).

not too late, the competent restorer will put a stop to this unhealthy juxtaposition and correct the faulty workmanship.

Unwarranted restoration: There is sometimes a very fine line separating ignorant blunders and an intention to deceive by falsifying or over-renovating a work of art that has naturally lost its freshness. Respect for a work of art comprehends respect for its ageing, respect for its format and indeed for everything that makes up its original character. Prints and drawings that have been trimmed, outrageously bleached or excessively restored are definitely compromised.

The conclusions to be drawn from these observations are that it is essential to be guided by the principle that restoration should be identifiable, durable and reversible.

ENDOGENOUS FACTORS
Paper carries within itself the causes of its own degenerescence. We have already seen that it is made up of other perishable substances besides cellulose fibres, principally, lignin, resin, loadings, glues, colorants and metallic impurities. The residues from the chemical treatments applied to paper pulp remain in it: chlorine, caustic soda, sodium sulphate, calcium bisulphide, among others. The more of these substances the paper contains, the more easily it deteriorates.

Hyperacidity of paper: Acidity is expressed in terms of pH on a scale of 1 to 14, varying from the most acid to the most alkaline, 7 being the neutral point. The acidity of paper is measured by means of an electronic pH meter or by the use of indicators, which colour when in contact with a wetted corner of the paper. The optimum pH for any paper used for graphic art, as too for mounts and boards, is between 6 and 7. Paper's natural hyperacidity or hyperacidity caused by the reaction of its constit-

32
Drawing on paper with traces of the adhesive used to hold it in its mount on the top border.

33
An album of drawings. The works of Victor Adam have been rearranged and bound.

uents with exterior chemical agents usually causes discoloration and a darkened appearance. Sooner or later the cellulose fibres will begin to break down.

The remedy for this condition is to deacidify the picture by painting it with or immersing it in an alkaline solution, or by using the solution in a vapour treatment.

Impurities and incrustations: As well as containing noxious chemical substances, paper has visible im-

purities or incrustations: fragments of wood-shav-
ings or iron-shavings (especially in hand-made
paper). We suggest mechanical extraction. Iron
stains that are left can be reduced by an application
of oxalic acid. This must be done quickly and
followed immediately by a thorough rinsing to
neutralize its corrosive action.

Decomposition of Strokes and Colours

Some drawing and colouring materials decay, cor-
rode or fade with time. This may happen spontaneously or be caused by the support or the conservation conditions.

Ink corrosion: Gallic acid transforms the iron sulphate in ferro-gallic inks into sulphuric acid which
eats away any part of the paper covered by a stroke
or wash, sometimes to the point of perforating it

34/35/36
Two-sided pen drawing. Here, too, the paper has been perforated by the lines of ink. It has been covered with mulberry
paper to preserve the verso. The first side, the second side and a
transparency are shown (Théodore Géricault).

(Figs. 34–36). Any paper covered by a drawing
done in a highly acid ink could eventually fall to
pieces, and it is therefore necessary to check and
correct the level of acidity of the ink in such works.
Where strokes have been badly eaten into the
picture should be lined (Fig. 37).

Flaking of gouache: If the binding agent used in
gouache and some watercolours begins to rot
because of ageing or drastic climatic changes, the
colour surface will flake. This cannot be completely
remedied, but its progress can be arrested: a vapour

50

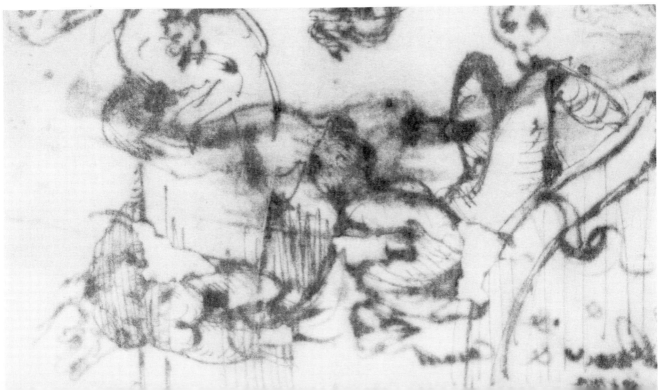

37
Pen drawing with a large gap caused by ink corrosion. The paper was lined and the largest empty space provided with a patch.

treatment will refix the size or the raised pigments can be soaked.

Degeneration of colours: There are many kinds of material other than white lead (Fig. 39) – pencil, chalk, watercolours, gouache, pastels – that can become transformed and fade, principally when exposed to light.
In our present state of knowledge, these changes are irreversible and irremediable.

38
Retouching a gap with a fine brush.

39
Watercolour with gouache, spotted with damp and showing ►► blotches in white areas (Charles Natoire, *Orpheus*).

METHODS OF RESTORATION

Despite their great variety the methods of the restorer can be grouped into a few basic techniques. The most common of these will be described here in detail.

Preparatory Work for Restoration

Most of the restorer's acts, including even the simplest (brushing, erasing, etc.), require drawings and engravings to be freed from any constraint imposed by the frames or mounts, as well as quirksome or erroneous methods of conservation such as folding, rolling up and multiple mounting.

These preparations require cautious and skilful handling, especially as certain features of the original mounting process may not be readily apparent. The restorer must be prepared to face, in spite of a disarming appearance of simplicity, unexpected difficulties, such as paper which is much more delicate than its appearance suggests or glue which is difficult to remove.

REMOVING THE FRAME

The elements of the frame (Fig. 40) are usually arranged as follows: the frame, in the restraining groove of which the glass is superimposed, the encircling window mount, the artwork and then the support. In some cases these pieces are joined together. Sometimes they are further consolidated by a thick piece of cardboard.

The first operation consists of taking the article apart. Usually an adhesive paper tape hides the nails and fasteners which hold the outside cardboard together on the back of the frame. Having loosened the tacks or other fasteners with a pointed instrument, one must then remove these with tweezers in order to extract the glass and free the various layers of cardboard which make up the mounting of the artwork.

It is advisable to proceed with caution; the work may be glued either to the window mount or to the support or to both at the same time. It is important not to encroach upon the delicate dismantling and unsticking procedures which will be described later.

UNFOLDING

Large format works (posters, geographical maps, architectural or decorative projects) are sometimes kept folded. In most cases these pieces are victims of a series of mishaps, negligences or simply difficulties of conservation. One must remember when starting to unfold works that this operation can be precarious, especially for fragile or old papers which have been kept for a long period of time in the same state. Particularly fragile materials (posters, tracings) will not survive many handling operations.

Therefore, before any step is taken, the restorer should bear in mind the methods of conservation likely to be used (even temporary ones), the restoration stages to follow, as well as the materials (heavy duty wrapping paper, fabric, hardboard, etc.) which will provide support to the work during restoration. It is advisable to work in a room without a draught and on a working surface large enough to hold the entire unfolded work. One cannot overemphasize the importance of carefully keeping any fragments which detach themselves from the original work.

UNROLLING

Rolled up artwork is often less fragile and so less damaged than folded works (except if it has been rolled up the wrong way or too tightly).

The same precautions should be taken when such works are to be spread out. Weights placed at the corners of the papers, or wherever it is appropriate, will counteract its tendency to roll up again, which can also be prevented by moistening the paper lightly, either by steaming or dampening, preferably on the back.

DIVIDING LARGE-SIZED WORKS

Large-sized works are sometimes composed of a number of sheets pasted together with overlapping edges, or edge to edge on a backing of paper or canvas. When they need restoring, it may be best to take them apart and treat each sheet separately. The restorer should try to separate them by removing the paste using dry methods or, if this fails, by dissolving the paste. This method, however, is frequently unsuccessful in difficult cases, and the restorer has to resort to cutting up the work with scissors or a sharp blade, following the line of any cuts which can already be seen on the surface of the print or drawing. Such drastic measures should only be taken if it is absolutely unavoidable. The restorer should always bear in mind that the work he has dismembered can only be re-assembled by complete re-lining. Other large-sized works are often fitted on a wooden stretcher. They are freed by cutting round them at the outer edge of the stretcher.

During these preliminary operations a suitable moment can be chosen to carry out disinfection and pesticide procedures (cf. Types of Treatment), to

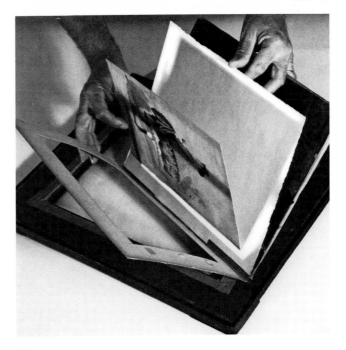

40
The components of a mount: the picture is fixed to its support by a horizontal hinge between the opening of the surround and the cardboard of the base.

avoid all risk of contaminating the material and its surroundings.

Dismantling (Removal of Supports and Linings)

When the drawings or engravings have been removed from their frames, put flat, unfolded or unrolled, one often finds that they no longer fit the supports so closely. When they have been badly fixed into position, the expansion of one or the other components causes an irregularity, or the

57

41
Pencil drawing of a landscape held by six spots of paste to its cardboard support. In slightly raking light traces of this process can be clearly seen (Auguste Jacques Regnier).

of moisture). Often, quite simply the choice of mounts does not suit the work. If the disharmonious mounting does not suit the work at all, the drawing or the engraving should be taken out of the support.

Dismantling is equally important when restoration rather than conservation work is contemplated. However, dismantling is sometimes neither advisable nor possible, particularly when the work is delicate or when the framing is of a very original or valuable type and should be preserved intact.
Inseparability of work from mounts can vary in extent, and one can encounter:

– *Multiple points of adherence:* the drawing or the engraving is fixed directly on its support in one or several places, at the corners for example, or fixed by hinges. One must be prepared to deal with a great diversity of adhesives (Fig. 41).

– *Adhesion over a surface area:* this is where the work is either directly glued all round its edges to the support and/or on to the window mount, or fixed to the support or mount by a sticky tape.

– *Complete cohesion or adherence:* the whole rear surface of the drawing is glued to the support. This is often the result of gross framing errors. It can also be the result of a particular method of mounting which is unique to a certain period, collector or master framer, in which case these techniques must be respected and the original idea preserved. It could also be the result of a restoration and conservation method called backing. This original restorative measure for fragile works must also be con-

cardboard or glues have undergone damage or degradation which has in turn affected the work (pitmarks, moulds, various permeations of seepages

served, especially if the risks are too great in renewing the backing support.

Dismantling is carried out using several techniques alternatively or simultaneously:

Manual Separation by Tearing Apart

When the paste is crumbling or aged, when the support is considerably weaker than the drawing or the engraving paper, and most particularly when hinges have been used, one can proceed manually to separate, by tearing apart, the various sections. The expression 'tearing apart' is perhaps misleading because this is an extremely delicate operation forbidding any clumsiness or haste.

The sheet of paper bearing the drawing must be placed flat on a smooth clean surface; this surface is

42
This two-sided pencil drawing was attached to its support with spots of paste which can still be seen on the verso. They can be removed by gentle washing (Jean-François Bosio).

the restorer's principal working area. It can be effectively provided in the form of a large marble or glass table. In any case the restorer must tear off the mount, the support or the fasteners from the drawing and not the reverse. *The most resistant part – or the least valuable part – must be the part which is pulled off.* The delicate or precious part must be kept fixed and immobile and thus safeguarded from rough action.

These important rules are valid for all separation work whether in dry or wet media. However, with pinpoint or partial adhesions (except when the drawing is unusually delicate), one can attempt firstly to separate the components by gently pulling the support from the artwork, bearing in mind the above-mentioned precautions.

Use of Tools

It is unusual for this first stage, when completed as described above, to appear perfect. There are generally at the very least the remains of paste and shreds of cardboard. There are some types of mounts which do not tolerate any form of separation, as when there are large glued areas or where the mount is pasted completely around the edges of the artwork. One must therefore resort to the use of special tools to cut or slice along the thickness of the cardboard. The best adapted tools are knives with a thin, flexible, sharp blade; lancets or scalpels or other small sharp blades. The blade needs to be inserted into the substance of the cardboard, around the edges of the pasted area of the drawing. Insert the blade one or two millimetres moving it carefully forward parallel to the surface. Then cut through the width of the cardboard so all that is left on the back of the drawing is a thin layer of cardboard bound by the glue. The remains of the paste and cardboard can be scraped off if necessary, then finally eliminated with the help of a damp cloth or solvent (Fig. 42).

One must not give way to the instinct to tug the drawing off the layer of paste or to insert the tool into the glue binding the support to the artwork. Such attempts would result in cutting right through the paper of the drawing or engraving, or in reducing its thickness.

These dry methods enable the restorer to complete most of the dismantling operation. Even when the drawing totally adheres to its support, he can try, especially if the support is made of *contrecollé* paper or compressed laminated cardboard, to pull off successive layers one at a time, leaving those which are in close contact with the back of the drawing. After trying all dry methods of removal, he should then resort to dissolution of pastes and glues. The types of glue used dictate the method of dismantling. Some pastes crumble, others are resistant to dry methods. It is preferable, despite the risks involved (providing the restorer proceeds with caution and patience), to dismantle works by dry methods (or at least first attempt to do so) rather than by wet methods or immersion.

However, supporting media such as canvas, wood, glass, metal or plastic do not bend easily during the process of manual separation. Nevertheless, canvas and plastic supports can be torn off relatively easily. One of the corners of the canvas or plastic film is lifted up while the paper of the drawing is kept firmly flattened; the canvas or plastic is then pulled and allowed to roll up on itself. For most types of stiff support, however, one has to resort to dissolving the adhesives either by partial treatment or by immersion, as we shall see further on.

Dry Methods of Cleaning

Most of the deterioration which attacks drawings or engravings affects them right through to the heart of the support; but others, such as dust, pencil or other coloured deposits, traces and specks of mildew are fairly superficial. Other marks requiring cleaning are only lightly ingrained among the fibres of the paper: incrustations, insect droppings, stains,

etc. A simple dry treatment for cleaning the surface removes from the drawing all such marks, which cloud details or obscure the paper. This preliminary treatment can be used for more difficult deteriorations (such as stubborn stains penetrating through the paper and stains and marks reaching above the surface). The residue has to be removed afterwards by more drastic methods.

The first step is to remove the work from its mount and place it flat on a smooth clean surface where it can be secured with one hand or with weights or clips. It is also useful to be able to turn the work over easily during cleaning.

The rules for the different dry methods of cleaning are as follows:

– *Proceed step by step:* Avoid working over too wide an area. It is advisable to work around the

43
Traces of erasing and scraping are removed with a soft brush.

drawn or coloured areas or to treat them very superficially.

– *Treat the surfaces uniformly:* Except when removing a stain or a series of stubborn stains, when one erases the surface of the work it is especially important not to concentrate too much on one area, as this is liable to destroy the harmony or unity of the piece.

– *Avoid too vigorous action:* This might tear or crease the sheet of paper or alter the texture of the surface in such a way as to produce a rough or grainy finish with particles which may become detached.

– *Do not forget the back of the work:* It is often useful to clean the back of a drawing or engraving when it is accessible. It is mandatory to do this when the stains or deterioration on the front are visible on the back.

BRUSHING

This is an elementary operation before any restoration is started when dealing with artwork that has been conserved in bad conditions and when the surfaces of the artwork is covered with a film of dust, mould or other types of residue.

Brushing should not, however, be confused with or substituted for disinfection or removal of parasites (undertaken at the dismantling stage), particularly when works could be contaminated.

The restorer must carefully dust or brush off the particles or mould, without spreading them over the work where they might become incrusted once more in the pores of the paper. The best adapted tools are soft brushes, light paintbrushes (Fig. 43) or cotton wool. Finally the restorer can blow gently over the surface of the paper with an insufflator. Large areas can be treated cautiously with a household vacuum cleaner.

ERASING

Erasing is efficient for eliminating more tenacious dust, reducing superficial stains, and removing traces of unwanted crayon (colouring, superfluous inscriptions, etc.).

The restorer can perfectly well use ordinary erasers if they are soft and clean. It is practical to sharpen them for more delicate jobs (Fig. 44). Powder erasers with which the paper surface is gently massaged are also recommended. Breadcrumbs kneaded into lumps can also be used, as in the days before the invention of erasers. In any case the restorer should refrain from using hard erasers (ink or typewriter types), which would be too abrasive. It would be superfluous to describe erasing in any more detail, but it is absolutely essential to remember that one must proceed with caution on small areas and brush off eraser residue from time to time (Fig. 45).

SCRAPING

Not all deposits which cover the paper surface or become incrusted in it are powdery or crumbling. Many of them are deposits on top of the paper. This is true of stains caused by paint, grease or candle wax and parasite waste matter.

Old papers also frequently contain fragments of oxidized iron, wood particles and unpulverized fibres, which alter their appearance.

When these incrustations are superficial, they can be extracted without causing any harm to the paper. This process consists of reducing the rough particles and deposits to the level of the paper surface, taking care to stop well before reaching this surface, or chipping off the crust which disintegrates and peels off.

44
When working close to the lines it is advisable to use an eraser cut to a point.

45
A fine brush picks up the traces of erasing and scraping.

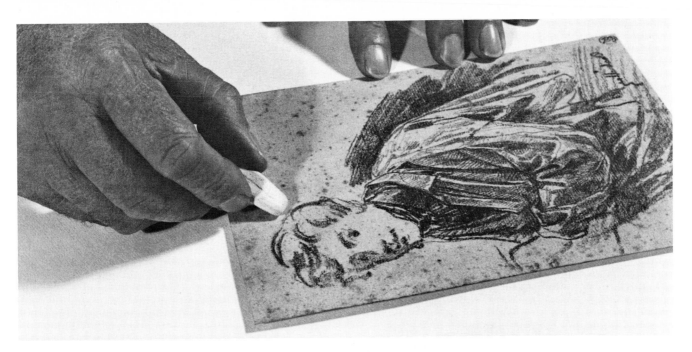

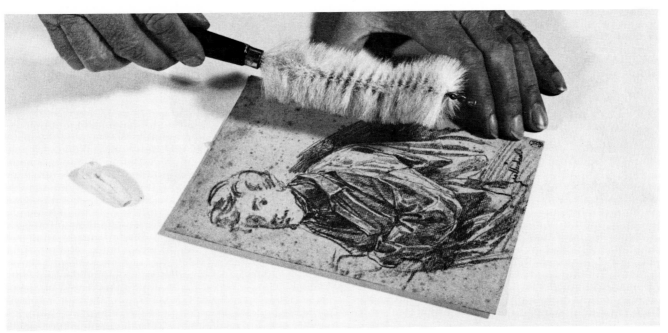

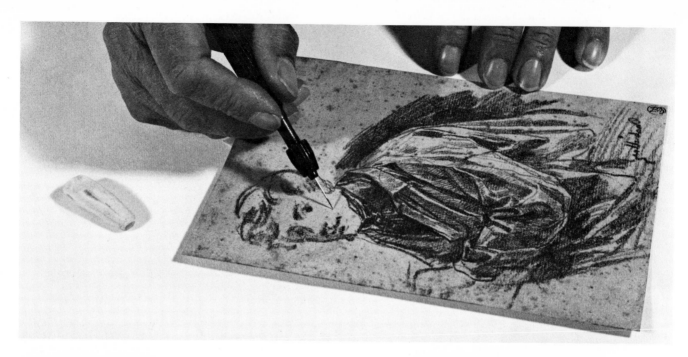

Usually the paper retains the imprint of the deposit or a trace of colour that must be removed by some other type of treatment.

The restorer uses a scraper, knife, scalpel, point or pin (Figs. 46 and 47). The electric eraser is an instrument for mechanical pouncing with various abrasives, which produces satisfactory results.

As a general rule, scraping and erasing operations appear misleadingly simple; the restorer should never be carried away by repetition of such mundane gestures and always remember that the object he is treating is a priceless work of art. By contrast, when these procedures are carried out correctly, they are virtually harmless to the items treated.

Partial Liquid Treatments

The operations described above were concerned directly and exclusively with surface damage and not with the supports and lines.

Partial or localized liquid treatments are more penetrating operations which eliminate damage but may alter the condition of the paper and the work of art. Results are, nevertheless, satisfactory provided the operator controls the transitory or durable changes that this treatment is liable to provoke:

– *Physical changes:* Water and most liquids expand paper and make it heavier. Alcoholic or acetone solutions, on the other hand, harden it without causing expansion. In general, liquid treatments cause variations in the elasticity of the paper which make it warp and buckle.

– *Chemical changes:* Certain solutions used for treatment (bleaching or stain removing) accelerate the dilution of size and alter the fibres of the paper, causing a permanent change in its structure.

– *Changes in appearance:* Even when treated in pure water, paper can change colour, and the periphery of the dampened area (Figs. 48 and 49) retains traces: haloes, mildew or circles.

These alterations can also affect the lines and colours of a work. They will be difficult and sometimes even impossible to reduce.

Treatments by complete immersion, which will be described further on, are risky and may, in a thorough restoration, endanger not only the damaged parts of the work but also those that are intact; local or partial treatments limit the risks, but through contrast show up the differences between the treated areas and the non-treated ones. Complete treatments should, therefore, be reserved for seriously or widely affected works (multiple stains and pricks, general perforation, serious or widespread mould, pasting all over, etc.). Small isolated stains on the paper surface, residues of localized glue spots, isolated staining and bleaching, and accidental oxidation of gouaches or chalks can be reduced by limited or superficial operations described here as partial liquid treatments.

In these treatments, the working surface generally coincides with the extent of the damage. Neverthe-

46
Encrustations are picked off with a needle or pin.

47
Remains of glue and the cardboard support are removed with a scraper.

48
◀ A solution of liquid on the surface of this watercolour has expanded the paper at this point and produced a depression which cannot be eradicated (photograph in slightly raking light).

49
▲ In a transparency the lighter area of paper formed by the localized moisture can be seen.

less, in certain cases it may be wise to include a particular area of the work: for example the margin, the background, the sky of a landscape or a clearly defined area. An inexperienced restorer, believing he can eliminate foxing distributed over the entire surface of a watercolour by treating each stain individually with a bleaching liquid, may produce light-coloured patches which destroy the paper's texture and attract the viewer's attention. The work to be treated should be free from any mount as far as possible and placed on a smooth clean surface. However, the restorer must be careful to keep it visible and accessible on both sides during the entire operation; it should in fact be possible to turn the work over to control the effects of treatment and continue it on the reverse side.

The use of a light-table is advisable when examining the work in transparency. Tools for this type of treatment are brushes, sponges, cotton wool and cotton buds for the application of solutions to the areas to be treated. A dropper is also used. Lastly, blotting paper is frequently needed, both to dampen the front and back of the work and to control the moisture.

Particular care must be taken to avoid all aforementioned disastrous accidents such as dark circles, haloes, warping, etc. To eliminate all residual moisture marks, the restorer can proceed by treating the reverse side of the drawing, taking care not to penetrate the paper, or by grading the amount of liquid he uses (i.e. using less and less as he moves away from the treated area). Finally, except when the reagent requires rinsing or neutralizing, the area to be treated can be impregnated very rapidly and dried immediately, with blotting paper for example.

Other devices can be contrived for limiting the effects of liquid treatment, in particular the use of masks cut out of cardboard, glass or plastic.

The general rules mentioned above can be applied to all types of limited liquid treatments; certain special points concerning them will be described in the following pages.

Removing Traces of Adhesives and Supports

We saw how unsticking by the dry process left

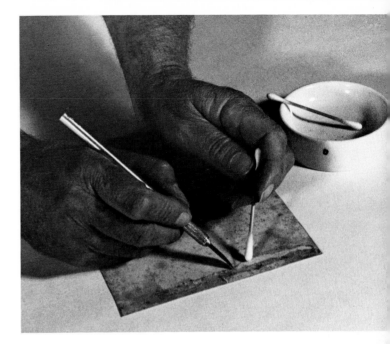

50
The removal of traces of paste and cardboard begins with dry processes and is completed after partial surface humidification (in this case, clean water applied with a cotton-wool stick).

traces of adhesive and cardboard. Partial or superficial moistening with a solvent appropriate to the type of adhesive may eliminate them completely (Fig. 50).

It must, however, be noted that when the adhesive

51
This pencil drawing has been damaged by exposure to light ▶ (note the impression of the window) and by impregnation with unsuitable pastes used in lining (Jean-Auguste-Dominique Ingres, *Portrait of the Engraver Calamatta*).

52
This drawing has had the lining removed, been bleached and ▶▶ then replaced in its mount.

Ingres a son
ami
Calamatta
1829.
Paris

Yngres à son
ami
Calamatta.

1828.

softens so does the paper; mechanical actions (scraping, tearing) connected with the damp method of dismantling must be undertaken with the greatest care, to avoid damaging the paper of the drawing or engraving.

Bleaching or Removal of Stains

Partial bleaching and removal of stains of any kind is advisable only when the bleaching agent or solvent does not require a thorough rinse. This limited treatment is particularly suitable for works which will not tolerate total immersion because of the fugacity of their medium (charcoal drawings, pastels, sepia washes, Far Eastern prints) or the fragility of their supports. Obviously this type of treatment makes the dilution or elimination of reagents a problem. This difficulty can, however, be overcome by briefly suspending their action with a controlled rinse or localized moistening between two pieces of blotting paper.

Re-whitening Highlights by Oxidation

It has been explained (cf. pp. 50–52) how the lead carbonate base of most white shades of gouaches, pastels and chalks can be transformed into brown or black lead sulphide (Figs. 53 and 54).

This very unsightly deterioration can easily be treated by a localized application of hydrogen peroxide.

It must be emphasized that this treatment is not harmful to the work if it is scrupulously limited to the lines or blackened surfaces and applied with care.

Thin brushes and cotton buds are especially suited to this task. The brush or stick is lightly dipped into the hydrogen peroxide and the affected areas mois-

tened (Figs. 56 and 57). The effect is rarely instantaneous; fresh applications are usually necessary. Blackened areas can also be eliminated with thin plaster plates or blotting paper soaked in hydrogen peroxide (cf. pp. 79–80). The chemical is rapidly and spontaneously eliminated; therefore, no rinsing is necessary.

After restoration the paper is placed under a press to remove any distortion caused by humidity. This operation can be confined to the treated areas. Pressing does not necessarily require a mechanical press. Except when dealing with three-dimensional works, the restorer can make up a pile of clean dry blotting paper (about 100 sheets) on a table, into the middle of which he can insert the drawing or engraving to be flattened. This procedure safeguards the lines made by the plate on the engravings, the grain or embossing of paper (mouldings, dry stamps, etc.). When such precautions are not needed, the pressure of the blotting paper can be increased by covering the pile with a wooden plank with weights evenly distributed on it.

Immersion Treatment

Soaking is a method which simultaneously takes care of every aspect of the work, involving not only any deterioration which requires restoration, but

53
Pen drawing heightened with blackened gouache. Detail before treatment.

54
Detail after treatment: the gouache has recovered its original whiteness.

70

also the components (paper, lines and colours) which are part of it.

It is, therefore, essential for the restorer to understand the tolerance level of the components and their resistance.

SELECTION OF WORKS
TO BE TREATED

Not all drawings or engravings lend themselves to treatment by immersion:

– *Condition of the work:* A drawing in very bad condition cannot withstand the shock of even a brief and carefully controlled soaking. Generally speaking, drawings in shreds, those with faded colours and lines, and those which cannot be removed from their mounts will be damaged rather than restored by this operation.

– *Fragility of the support:* Even when they are well preserved, certain works, through the composition of their supports, cannot tolerate prolonged immersion. Poor quality fibre paper can dissolve in liquid or at all events become dangerously softened. Synthetic supports decompose in the solvent.

– *Fugacity of lines and colours:* A single immersion, and even more a soaking for stain removal and bleaching, causes a varying degree of weakening of the colour and strength of the work treated.

The materials used by the artist withstand this weakening process differently according to their type. With a few exceptions, oily engraving inks, Indian ink, black chalk, red chalk and lead crayon withstand immersion and most treatments.

Sepia washes, recent watercolours, charcoal drawings, chalk drawings, pastels and the light inks of Japanese engravings can be greatly damaged by liquid treatments.

Between these two extremes there are materials which can tolerate such treatment with due care; this is true of gouaches and old watercolours, stump-brush drawings and even certain well-fixed pastels.

– *Handling difficulties:* The dangers and difficulties of the immersion treatment can oblige the restorer to abstain from undertaking it on works of outsize format or on ones which are awkward to handle, such as long cylindrical drawings, or works of a size exceeding the capacity of the equipment available. Liquid treatments prove that there is no restoration without danger. Selecting the right treatment involves a choice, sometimes final, between the advantages and disadvantages which the restorer must know how to calculate. He is helped in this by experience and experimentation. Experience cannot be improvised. It is therefore advisable, before any immersion treatment, to proceed by testing a small fragment of the work or possibly a similar sample with the same deteriorations and a trace of the materials used by the artist. This test will reveal the viability of the possible solutions and the reactions of the paper.

55
The lead carbonate base of the white gouache has turned into black lead sulphide in places. The oxydized parts turn black in the clouds and the outlines of trees and faces (Pierre-Clément Marillier).

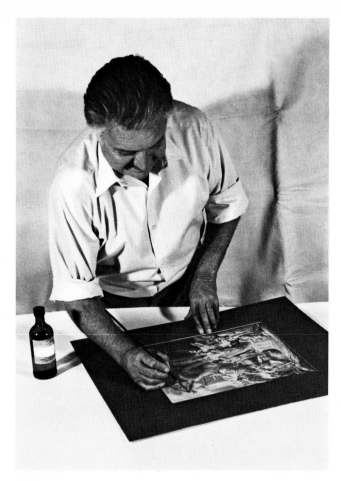

56/57
A brush is lightly dipped in hydrogen peroxide and stained areas are moistened.

Preparation of the Work

When the diagnosis is complete and it appears that the work can be treated by immersion, it must be prepared for this. The work should be freed from mounts as far as possible. This precaution is particularly important here as any foreign body on the paper of the drawing (lining, mounting, remains of adhesive or cardboard) could hinder the control and progress of the treatment.

Foreign bodies could obstruct the penetration of the liquid and its reagents, which must operate regularly and uniformly.

On the other hand, in order to assist the drawing or engraving to withstand the profound physical and chemical changes which assail it on immersion, it must be rested on a *support*, which must be resistant, supple and transparent.

One can choose between sheets of tracing paper or cardboard, pieces of fabric, nylon or canvas, or even sheets of glass or Perspex, according to the qualities required of this support. Care must be taken that the reagent does not attack or dissolve the support. The drawing, resistant or fragile, will be laid on this prop or inserted between two supports.

Equipment

Equipment and experience are what make the difference between the professional and the amateur. For a treatment by immersion, a whole range of containers and apparatus can be used, ranging from a simple plate to fixed laboratory baths. Everything depends on the size of the works to be treated and the frequency of operations.

Plastic, glass or china containers, as used by photographers or chemists, can be put to good use. It is most inadvisable to work directly in a basin, sink or bath, where the drawing might become damaged by running water or the force of the water going down the drain hole. However, it appears reasonable to work near a fixed installation providing a water supply and disposal of used liquids.

The container should be slightly larger in size than the work and shallow, so that the restorer can economize on the treatment liquid while at the same time maintaining easy handling. When the operation involves several soakings, it is advisable to use several containers placed side by side rather than to fill and empty the same container repeatedly. When the size of a work exceeds the dimensions of all receptacles, immersion methods can be attempted by rolling the works up on supports.

Ideally one should have ready a small tool to perform localized operations (brush or cotton bud), stimulating or concentrating the reagent's effect, or (flat knives) to eliminate the remainder of clinging glue or cardboard.

Immersion

There are several methods of submerging the drawing and its support in the treatment bath (Fig. 58). When the drawing is intact and able to tolerate immersion, one first lays the support on the bottom of the container. The drawing is then put on the surface of the liquid and allowed slowly to sink down as it soaks up the liquid; if necessary slight pressure is exerted with the palms of the hands (Fig. 59).

When the drawing is fragile, the restorer is advised to introduce it with its supports, pushing it diagonally into the liquid. Care must be taken that fragments do not loosen with movements of the liquid and that any tears are not worsened by fluid pressures while the submerged drawing is being moved. A noteworthy and ingenious method, used particularly by the restorers of the Bibliothèque Nationale, consists of floating the engraving on the surface of the bath whilst at the same time resting it on a wooden frame stretched on a nylon trellis. In this way the work is gently impregnated in the treatment solution without risking the accidents described above (Fig. 60).

Except for one or two rare cases, the solution is harmless to the skin. It is, therefore, preferable to carry out these immersions directly by hand, without using tools that might harm the paper (pincers, blades, brushes) or gloves that dull the sense of touch.

Control and Supervision of the Soak/Bath

Whatever the precision of the preceding tests and of the established programme, control of treatment must be strict and continuous. The duration of the immersion, even though estimated according to previous experiment, will vary according to the type of paper, its thickness, age, condition, and obstacles encountered by the liquid and reagents, as well as under the influence of an infinity of other parameters.

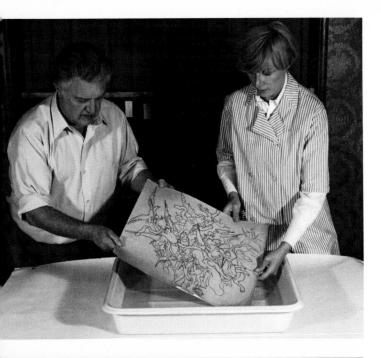

Careful observation of the progress of the treatment is the only way to guard against untoward occurrences. The treatment must be stopped immediately the desired results are obtained. It is essential *not to prolong these operations needlessly* since they are always harmful. It is particularly important never to leave the drawing for several hours unattended. At the first sign of unwanted or unexpected change, or at the first sign of excessive alteration in the paper or lines, the treatment must be stopped immediately. It is always preferable not to finish the bleaching or removal of the stain rather than to compromise the survival of a work of art.

Sometimes it is more prudent to interrupt the treatment before the end result is achieved. The restorer can thus anticipate the effects of the reagent, which continue after removal from the bath and only cease after the reagent is removed by rinsing, neutralizing or drying.

Completion of Treatment

The drawing is extracted from the bath by lifting up the support on which it is resting in order to avoid putting any pressure on the damp paper (Fig. 61). In most cases the simplest method consists of holding between the thumb and forefinger of each hand the two corners of the support pulling it out diagonally with the drawing adhering to the support, allowing the surface water to flow off gently without any

58
When dealing with a large drawing, an assistant will be needed to support the work at several points. A drawing is shown being placed obliquely into the treatment bath.

59
The drawing is submerged with the flat of the hand.

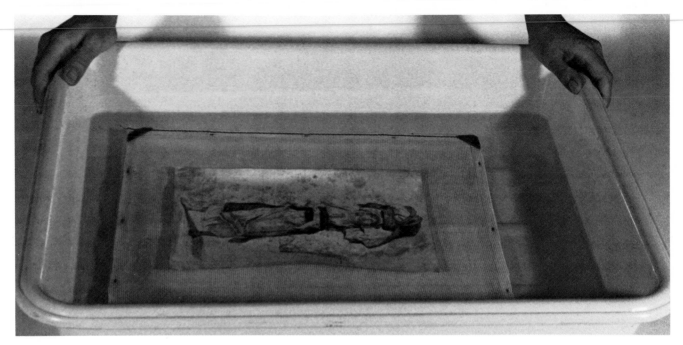

shaking (Fig. 62). When the drawing is large, it can be held at various points by an assistant to steady the support.

If other treatment baths are involved and if there are contra-indications, the work can be plunged immediately into the next bath. Not until the sequence of treatments is completed can one proceed to drying. This must be done in two parts. The work is transported – attached to its support – and turned on to a blotting paper to rest. The support can then be detached with delicate handling. After excess humidity has evaporated, the work, while still damp, is gently pressed between two large piles of blotting paper using only moderate pressure.

Particular Methods of Handling Certain Immersion Baths

Some baths require special instructions:

60
An ingenious technique consists of floating a wooden frame strung with a lattice of nylon on which the work rests. It is lightly impregnated without the risk of total immersion.

– *Impregnation baths:* It may be necessary to immerse in water either a piece of paper, a print, or a drawing before pressing or packing it, the object being to expand the work uniformly. Immersion is relatively short in this case and stopped as soon as the work has been completely immersed.

– *Deacidification baths:* The object is to neutralize any acidity of the paper (cf. pp. 48–49). The immersion is also interrupted as soon as the sheet is completely immersed. The products used are often dangerous.

– *Cleansing baths:* It is to be noted that a simple bath of pure water eliminates superficial dust from most drawings and also attenuates unwanted

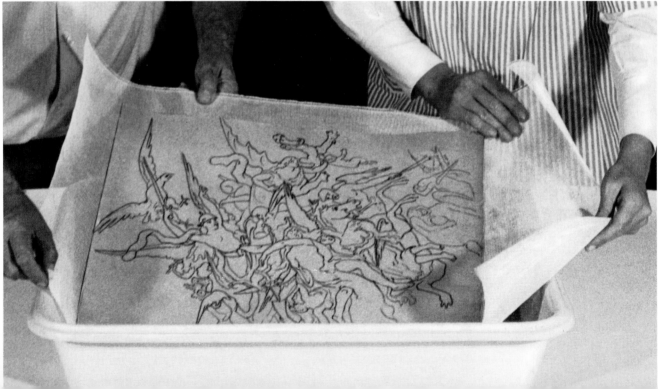

marks. This preliminary cleaning revives the paper.

– *Baths which loosen adhesives:* These are cold baths of pure water (no hotter than 50 °C/122 °F). Their aim is ito remove any traces of soluble glue as well as to free tenacious backings stuck with these adhesives. The immersion procedures and subsequent brushing and scraping of damp paper must be done with great care on the surfaces of the dampened paper.

– *Baths used for sizing and re-sizing:* These are to stiffen the paper and will be described in detail further in the text.

– *Tinting baths:* These baths of coloured liquid are used to tint or retint patches or sheets of paper. It is advisable to deploy the baths successively – each immersion followed by a complete drying, only then can you safely judge if you are close to the desired tint of the samples or models.

– *Bleaching baths:* The operating sequence can be split up as follows: a dampening bath precedes the bleaching bath, the strength of which must have been carefully measured with a graduated gauge, the temperature measured and the duration regulated. It will be followed by a rinsing bath in gentle running water lasting at least an hour to completely wash out the reagent used. A neutralizing bath between two rinses could help complete the washout of bleach.

61
The drawing is lifted from the bath by raising the support on which it lies, thus avoiding any strain or pull on the softened paper.

62
The drawing must be lifted from the bath by raising the support in such a way that the liquid runs off freely without any backwash.

– *Baths which remove impregnated material or devarnish:* Their use is to extract, with the help of solvents, foreign substances incorporated or added to the paper. Solvents must exactly suit the nature of the matter to be extracted yet not harm any of the components of the work.

– *Baths for removal of stains:* Stain removers and other solvents can be applied during an immersion. One can make a local application to the sheet of paper still submerged in the bath, or preferably one can apply the remover after momentarily extracting the work from the bath by means of its support. This procedure enables one to concentrate the treatment on certain specific points whilst at the same time diffusing or neutralizing its effects. It is thus possible to use several reagents during one operation.

Other baths, even with their own particular methods, can be easily carried out using the aforementioned description. These treatments, however, require a great deal of experience, and each one of them should be well tested beforehand.

Types of Treatment

Works which could not tolerate the inherent trauma caused by liquid or mechanical interventions can sometimes be submitted to less strenuous types of treatment, which however require more technical facilities; these include gaseous treatments, through evaporation or vaporization.

These methods also permit treatment in depth of major deteriorations without ruining the structure of the damaged object.

TREATMENTS IN GASEOUS ENVIRONMENT

Sterilization, disinfection, insect destruction and general elimination of biological elements harmful to the paper, is achieved by the action of the gas or vapours inside airtight cases or vacuum pans.

One starts by evaporation, or sublimation of bacterial products, fungicides or insecticides or by permeation with gas. This operation is carried out either at room temperature or by increasing the temperature inside the airtight cases. It can be done under normal or low pressure conditions.

Bleaching, removal of stains and even expanding the paper can be done by evaporation in a closed environment.

These techniques are taken from well known restoration methods for archives and books where they are in current usage.

BY EVAPORATION

The same effect can be obtained by simple evaporation, in the open, of liquids and treating substances in contact with or near the paper of the drawing or engraving.

Delicate sheets of paper can be sterilized by placing them between two pieces of tissue paper impregnated with fungicide or by placing them on a permeable support (nylon net) above a solid article (a piece of material, or plaster of Paris) saturated with the appropriate compound.

A sheet of paper hung at an appropriate distance over a bucket of boiling water will expand as easily as it would if immersed.

BY VAPORIZATION

Vaporization is the projection on to the object to be treated of a liquid under gas pressure. For this purpose one uses compressors or aerosols. For small operations one can use vaporizers – or aerographs – with a mouth piece or a bulb.

This procedure is unsatisfactory for removal of stains, bleaching and sterilization but is particularly adapted to surface treatment operations, fixing (of pastels, charcoals and gouaches), varnishing, tinting and removal of size and re-sizing.

THROUGH CONTACT

Finally many stain removal operations can be successfully carried out, without putting the paper of the drawing or engraving under any mechanical constraint, by employing absorbing powders or 'absorbent solvent' materials. Absorbent powders are simply applied to the paper's surface – recto and verso – directly on to stains. Talc and fuller's earth deal efficiently with recent grease stains. Household cleaning products include various dry substances for cleaning made of rice powder, which act by absorption. Some of these can be used satisfactorily to remove stains from papers. Nevertheless, the restorer should test, with much caution, against the likelihood of damage by these materials before applying them to works of art. One can complete the treatment with the help of liquid solvents.

In any case the catalogue of restoration procedures can be prolonged without limit according to the ingenuity and science of those who practice it. However ingenious they may be, methods which only apply to particular cases have not been enumerated here.

Sizing Techniques

Sizing operations are frequently required in restorative work.

This can be explained firstly by the presence of size as an essential constituent of paper; ageing, accidental damage or over-energetic treatments which paper may have undergone result in a considerable deterioration of the paper by removing from it this element, which is necessary for its firmness. The restorer must, therefore, reconstitute the 'body' of the paper by replacing the size.

However, even if the freshness of the paper remains intact, the fragility of these graphic works will often oblige the restorer to consolidate them by pasting them on to a more durable support. Since artists often use light and fragile materials, there is a corresponding tendency to conserve these works and present them by pasting them into albums, on to mounts, or on simple linings.

Even if this method of care is suitable, it does not justify the restorer constantly having a brush of paste in his hand and daubing here and there. One must remember that only seriously and obviously deteriorated drawings that have also become weakened should be treated in this way. Work which is in no danger does not require abusive and excessive sizing or backing. If the benefits of this treatment have been proved, it nevertheless demands a considerable transformation of the work which must not be underestimated and which necessitates certain precautions:

– *Sizes* should resemble as closely as possible the original sizes constituting the paper; they must give a genuine guarantee of conservation and adherence.

– *Strengthening and reinforcing materials* will be identical or similar to the paper of the period or, in default, will be modern paper of the best quality.

SIZING AND RE-SIZING

Re-sizing is the operation by which the restorer reconstitutes the surface binding of the paper which has been lost due to damage or treatment. Sizing is the same operation applied to paper naturally weak in size (as is frequently the case for prints).

One proceeds by re-impregnating the paper with size, usually treating it in a sizing solution. This solution can be sprayed on the surface of the paper, recto and/or verso, or applied with a brush.

We saw previously how to operate the baths (cf. pp. 75–79). Sizing by spraying or by brush show a similarity to partial liquid treatments (cf. p. 65). In these last two cases it is advisable to avoid excessive and irregular deposits of size, which would detract from the smooth plane of the paper.

Drying is achieved either by hanging the drawing up on a wire or by laying it flat on blotting paper, where it is kept weighted in position as soon as it ceases to be tacky or adhesive.

Sizing operations can be readily repeated, and this enables the restorer to proceed with caution and control apparent results. Nevertheless, twenty-four hours is a suitable time to let the paper lie and rest between operations.

Preparation or Finish

Certain works are executed on 'finished' paper. This finish is a coating, usually with a paste base, applied to the surface of the paper and imparting a particular appearance or colour. A large number of drawings of the fifteenth century were executed in silverpoint technique on paper coated with bone powder. The preparation or finish undergoes the same deterioration as the sizing in the paper. To restore this finish, which is essential to the appearance of the work, the restorer must be able to analyse it and reconstitute it. He will then apply the substitute finish to the surface of the paper, usually with the aid of a brush.

Paper Pulp

When the loss of sizing has resulted in the destruction of the paper and the appearance of gaps, one can restore the paper over limited areas by applying portions of paper pulp. This procedure can also be used to fill up holes caused by worms.

This paper pulp consists of a maceration of cellulose fibres in water. To use it, this pulp is mixed with a vegetable-based size – including possibly a dye. It is then applied to the defects in the paper by means of a fine spatula, with care being taken not to over-fill the defects as the pulp is smoothed over the surface. Libraries, archives and institutes of restoration have laboratories with machines which carry out this operation mechanically. The results, although usually satisfactory, rarely satisfy the safety standards and the appearance desired in the restoration of works of art.

Repairing of Tears

Size is also used, of course, to glue back pieces of paper. The restorer can repair most tears that occur accidentally on drawings or engravings by sticking back the flaps of the tear. However fine, the paper never gets torn in a straight clean edge, and the irregularities of the tear permit the glue to hold and allow a certain overlap of the jagged edges.

After ensuring that the two edges are perfectly matched and do not have any gaps nor parts jutting out, the restorer coats the edges with sizing paste over a 1–2 millimetre width and then applies one edge on top of the other and removes any surplus glue with a damp sponge. This work is carried out on a flat surface, on blotting paper for example. The restored drawing is kept in a press during the drying.

Partial Backing

If the tear is not made good by the procedure described above, either because it is too large or because the edges do not adhere, one can reinforce the edges by sticking a narrow band of mulberry paper on the back of the drawing. Here too sizing paste is used, taking care that it is sufficiently thick not to wet the drawing excessively.

In this way the restorer can repair with pieces of mulberry paper or other types of paper that have been carefully 'bevelled' around the edges tears around the outside or gaps in the middle of the work. It is obvious that major accidents cannot be treated by this method.

BACKING OR LINING PROCEDURES

Backing is the method of glueing the complete surface of the drawing or engraving on to a support. This very frequent operation indisputably gives tired paper a new life, smoothnness and firmness. However, lining hides the reverse side of the work and causes watermarks, inscriptions and sometimes even another drawing to disappear. For this reason some would query the worth of the procedure. Preservation of all the original signs of a work is imperative for the restorer. However, safeguarding the work is even more important. When the work can be protected without backing, the restorer will always prefer to maintain it in its original state. Each time that its protection requires a backing, the restorer will apply one, ensuring at the same time that all interesting marks remain visible.

Whatever method is used, the backing procedure requires certain precautions, as it is practically irreversible; even if the chosen adhesive is easily soluble, once the drawing is backed, it will rarely endure removal from its backing without becoming damaged. This arises from its fragility. The main expedient is to choose the backing paper very carefully; it is reasonable, for example, to back an old drawing on paper of similar age (of the same period, or if possible from the same manufacturer). The grain of the paper and its watermark should not show too indiscretely. But it is important that the colour of the antique paper and that of the new backing, as well as its grain, should match and that line marks should not be at a different angle.

Also, generally speaking, the supporting paper should perform its role efficiently. It must be more resistant – although not thicker than the paper of the drawing; a thin mulberry paper is sometimes as useful as a thick heavy paper.

It should be emphasized, that the use of cardboard for an entire backing is totally inadvisable.

Procedures Using Stretched Backing

The paper chosen as support or backing is dampened on both sides by immersing it for a few seconds in water or by moistening it using a sponge.

When it has sufficiently expanded, it is placed on a piece of flat wood or glass which is considerably larger (Fig. 63). Strips of sticky tape 4–8 centimetres wide are stuck around the edges so as to stick partly to the paper and partly to the wood or glass surface (Fig. 64). In drying the paper will stretch under great tension. The restorer can then paint the glue on to this supportive paper on the places destined to hold the drawing as well as on the back of the drawing itself (Fig. 65).

The drawing or engraving is then put on that part of the expanded paper which is ready to receive it (Fig. 66). If the drawing is sufficiently strong, it is transferred by itself, but if it is in a poor condition or very softened, one transfers it with its backing/support.

Once the drawing is in place, it can be flattened and any pockets or air bubbles eliminated by pressure with the palm of the hand, taking care to use an intercalated, thin sheet of paper (Figs. 67 and 68). The pressure can be increased by using a damp sponge or a cold iron.

These operations require experience and masterful handling. For example, if the drawing cannot be allowed to slide on the glue without being damaged, some restorers will hold the board up vertically so that, having applied the top glued edge of the paper, it can be allowed to fall down by degrees. When the whole article is quite dry (after about a week), the backing paper is cut level with the strips of adhesive in order to free it from the wooden board or the glass pane. Though the drying process may seem lengthy, the restorer is strongly advised not to try to speed the process by placing the work in an excessively dry atmosphere.

This procedure, which is the most common, can be

applied generally to drawings with backs which do not present any interesting features or stamps.

Other Methods of Stretched Backing

The method just described is the basis of most resticking operations. One can, in fact, superimpose one or several other sheets of paper on the stretched backing before fixing the drawing. This superimposition reinforces the lining or permits the setting up of a mount. This is the way that master mounters used to work: they lined the drawing with several thicknesses of paper (four or five), then decorated its edges with strips of tinted paper on which they traced filigree and other decorations and scrolls (Fig. 69). This method is also applicable to creases, undulations or swellings affecting the drawings or engravings which have not been reduced by pressing.

One proceeds in the same way for lining on a stretched backing, the difference being that the drawing itself is dampened and edged with sticky tapes. After drying, lasting also about a week, the drawing is cut level with the stays of the tape. It will have regained all its flat surface, but lost a narrow part around its periphery.

Backing Methods Using Pressure

Pasting under pressure is also widely used, especially for small sheets of paper or for lining on mulberry paper or fabric. It has the advantage of being faster, but it requires the use of a paper press.

The restorer puts the face of the drawing on a smooth clean surface and coats the reverse side evenly with glue, smoothing it out with a thick brush. One side of the paper chosen for the backing is also coated with glue, or just dampened. The backing sheet is then put on the glued back of the drawing. The contact between these sheets of paper is increased by pressure with the palm of the hand through an intercalated paper. The whole article is then put under the press between two piles of blotting paper, after removing any excess glue with a slightly damp sponge.

The pressing should last as least as long as the drying.

Backing Works with Two Sides

We have said that the restorer will not be happy if the inscriptions and markings found on the back of a drawing, or its watermark, disappear. However, the sacrifice of one of two drawings is even less acceptable when the work is double faced.

When backing is thought to be indispensable for the survival of the work, there are only two solutions (Figs. 70–72).

a. Use of Classical Backing Techniques

They consist of backing the drawing using a stretched backing or under a press, choosing as supportive material some thin, transparent or translucent but strong support. The most frequently used are mulberry papers, tissue papers with a fine-grained weave and certain transparent papers. Without making it a firm rule, backings using paper

63
The sheet of paper selected for a support is damped on both sides with a sponge. It lies on a considerably larger wooden board.

64
Strips of gummed or glued paper 4 cm wide are attached round the edges, partly on the paper and partly on the wooden board.

are done by stretching, and backings with fabric are for preference done with a press.

Legibility of the reverse side will not be perfect. The restorer, aware of this imperfection, must choose which side he wants to show to advantage.

b. Lamination Techniques and Their Application

Lamination is a procedure used to reinforce documents in archives. Briefly, it consists of sealing the page of a document between two films of cellulose acetate or some similar plastic material at a high temperature and under strong pressure. The institutes for book restoration and most archives have machines called 'Laminator' or Barrow machines, named after the inventor. These carry out lamination of sheet documents at a temperature of 160 °C/320 °F between two rollers exerting a pressure of 20–140 kilogrammes per square centimetre on the acetate films.

A preliminary application of this procedure is to superimpose on the acetate films on both sides a sheet of transparent paper or a sheet of natural silk. This procedure can theoretically satisfy the requirements for backing graphic works on one or both sides. However, the use of a substance so alien to the components of paper causes a fundamental change in its appearance. This treatment may, therefore, appear acceptable for consolidating and conserving archive documents and, if absolutely necessary, for posters or ruined works; but it is difficult to accept for the repair of works of art.

Lamination has many other applications, and there are certain variants which better satisfy scientific criteria for restoration of works of art. It has, in particular, provided the answer to the apparently impossible task of separating a sheet widthwise. This method is called 'exfoliation'; though obviously the most sophisticated answer, it may not be the most advisable for the problem of drawings on both sides of the same sheet of paper.

To obtain this result, after the usual lamination procedures (between two sheets of tissue paper sealed to the drawing by an acetate film), one separates these two films, to which then remain attached on one side the front and on the other the reverse of the drawing. These two half-sheets are then coated with a sizing paste. Each of them is backed on to a paper support, as in classical type backings, or one can interpolate between these two pre-sized half-sheets a reinforcement paper. After drying under a press, the operation is completed by plunging the reconstituted drawing or the two separate halves of the drawing into an acetone bath which will dissolve the acetate coating while sparing the sizing paste. The paper will almost resume its natural appearance, but the work will more often than not have lost some of its originality and aesthetic quality.

65
The backing sheet and the back of the drawing are then coated with paste.

66
The drawing is moved with the help of a tracing paper support to the right position. It should be noted that one side is placed on the board first, so that it is perfectly aligned.

PATCHING PROCEDURES

Patches are pieces of material (usually paper) used to cover up gaps in a work or to make good a missing part (Fig. 73). It is a grafting procedure. As for all grafts, it is carried out by 'grafts' taken from

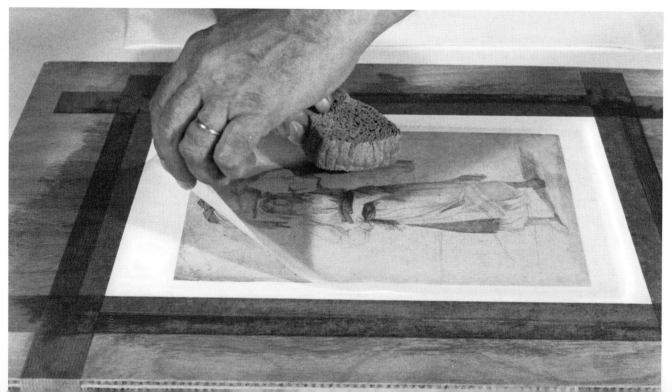

the article itself or supplied from another object.
The restorer can take a marginal fragment of paper
from the work to ensure the best match in grafting.
These are the most successful patches.

If it is not possible to scrounge a small part of the

69
Corner of an old mount showing the mounter's impression.
Note that at the corners are the holes made by a dry point used
to mark the position.

70
This pen drawing on paper is double-sided. Because the paper is ▶
so strong, it has been possible to place it on a sheet of old paper
fixed in the opening of an empty surround (seventeenth-century
Italian school, *The Education of Christ*).

67/68
◀ The drawing is laid down and all air pockets and bulges
smoothed out, first with the palm of the hand and then using
stronger pressure applied with a damp sponge. The restorer
then removes the protective tracing paper.

71
On a transparency the drawing on the back can be seen under ▶▶
double light.

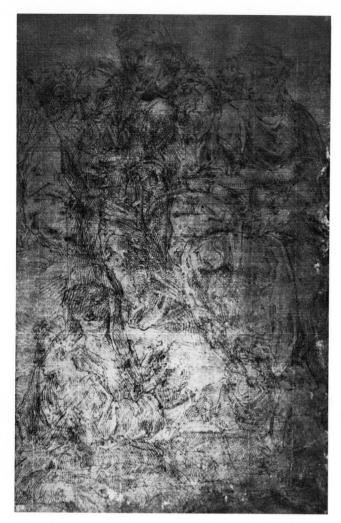

72
The drawing on the back, seen in a transparency.

Patching on Backed Sheets

In most cases works with breaks in them are so fragile that the restorer has backed them. The restoration of these gaps comes after the work has been backed.

The piece is cut from the fragment of paper chosen after the shape of the gap has been carefully drawn on it (directly by transparency or by using tracing paper [Figs. 74 and 75]).

The position of the gap and the reverse side of the patch are lightly coated with sizing paste and the piece is applied to the gap (Fig. 76). The work is dried under a press and then, if necessary, the parts jutting out are trimmed off with a razor blade or scalpel. Finally the restorer is left with the possibility of making good the actual parts of the drawing missing because of the gap (Fig. 77).

Patches on Unbacked Sheets

These operations are also carried out on works which, although damaged, do not require lining.

In this case the patch is stuck to and gets support from the edges of the gap, preferably from the reverse side. Consequently, the edges of the patch will overlap by one or two millimetres those of the gap. One then bevels very gently around the patch and the gap and coats them with size. The glued pieces are then pressed meticulously to the work with the help of a bone paper-knife through an interposed sheet of paper, and then the work is put under the press. The choice of paper for patches for non-backed works is a delicate matter because any difference in the coefficient of expansion between the paper of the original and the paper of the patch results in buckling around the restored area.

drawing, or if its removal assumes the proportion of an amputation, one must find a sample of paper as nearly similar as possible, with the same qualities and characteristics as the paper of the drawing. The success of patching carried out in this way depends entirely on the similitude of the piece added.

92

Re-Margining

These are operations by which one artificially enlarges the size of a drawing or engraving by the addition of a margin in a single piece around the whole periphery of the edge. The restorer proceeds in the same way as for setting pieces of loose paper, limiting the overlap on the reverse to a narrow band of a few millimetres. Here again the choice of paper must give the impression that the work is intact.

Window Mounting

These collage mounts are used each time that one wishes to display the work (with one or two faces) using only a very slight hold around the edges. The procedure allies itself to re-margining, as a window mount is likewise pasted around the edge of the work. This pasting can be done on either the front or the reverse face. The added piece does not have to be of the same material, but it must expand and contract identically with the paper of the work, thus avoiding excessive tension. It is inadvisable, therefore, to use window mounting for drawings on delicate paper (tracings, thin or old paper).

Restoration of Lines and Colours

The last stage of restoration is the reconstruction or 're-integration' of gaps in the work. It can only be undertaken after the basic materials have been restored to the best possible condition.

Its success is a matter of talent rather than technical expertise. Ethical considerations too must be taken into account. One cannot help noticing the difference in the attitude of the restorer who works for public bodies and the one who works for a clientele of private collectors or dealers. The former are sometimes over-cautious while the latter take too many risks.

Nevertheless, there are certain strict rules which ought, in the author's opinion, to guide all restorers, and these will be set out here.

73
Pencil drawing on tracing paper. The drawing has been pasted down and shows a small hole (Alfred Grevin, *Portrait of Victorien Sardou*).

93

Restoration should never be used as a substitute for treating damage.

Among the causes of deterioration of graphic art some are accidental, but others are closely allied to the materials of which the work is composed and the conditions in which it is kept. The restorer should never attempt to cover up the effects of this type of damage but should seek out the cause and eradicate it.

Only when every restorative measure has been exhausted should the restorer resort to disguising irreparable damage, e.g. by unobtrusive and limited retouching. In extreme cases, such as a single indelible greasy patch in the middle of a face, it may be covered with a coat of gouache or a skin of paper; but these examples should be regarded as exceptions to the rule.

Restoration should be limited to reconstruction of damaged sections of the work.

Restoration is not re-creation. The restorer's aim should be to mitigate the detrimental effect of gaps and stains on the appearance of a work.

He should never set out to recompose a work or to execute it afresh starting from the remaining traces of the original, with the unavowed intention of deceiving the spectator. He will, therefore, avoid all excess personal interpretation and decorative touches and confine himself strictly to unobtrusive restoration.

Restoration of a work of art must never entail any deception; it should be discernible. Unlike the forger who attempts to take over from the artist, the restorer modestly reconstructs lines and colours. He only wants his contribution to make the work look acceptable, not to defy analysis. Indeed, some resto-

rations can be executed satisfactorily by reducing the contrast between intact and damaged areas. An unobtrusive wash of Indian ink, for example, will have the same effect as the lines of an etching; it is an effective substitute for the laborious reconstruction of these lines.

Restoration should be reversible as far as possible.

One of the greatest achievements of restoration and the study of art history is undoubtedly that of teaching the restorer to look upon his own contribution with humility.

He has no mandate to compete with the creator of the work or to substitute himself for the artist, let alone to tamper with original work to display his own prowess. He should always bear in mind, when embarking on radical treatment of a badly damaged piece, that a future restorer may perhaps be able to do better by applying a new but less drastic process. This principle should be his guide in every stage of restoration work, but especially when he is reconstructing lines.

74
The outline of the hole is reproduced on similar paper – in this case, tracing paper.

75
The patch is cut out with scissors.

76
The area to be patched and the back of the piece are lightly pasted, and the patch is placed in the gap.

77
The last stage is the restoration of the lines broken by the hole.

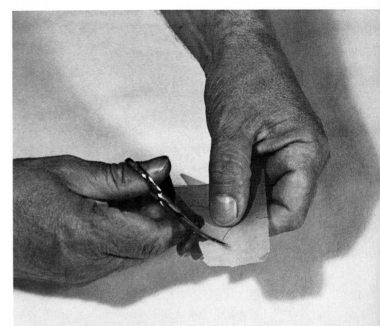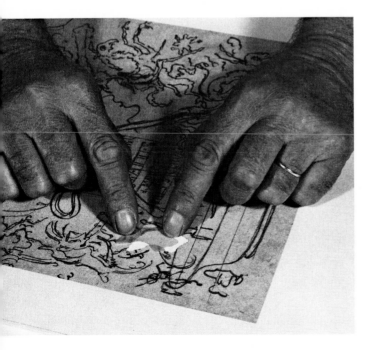

Reconstructed parts must harmonize with the original or with the style of the original in cases where nothing survives.

We have seen how important it is to establish an accurate record of the condition of a work before embarking on restoration. The photograph or tracing of the original is an invaluable guide in reconstructing lines.

Unfortunately, these records are usually an insufficient guide to the composition of missing passages. If it is decided that the restoration will be attempted despite this, the restorer should use a work in the same style as a guide.

In the same spirit of fidelity to the original — needless to say — the restorer should use the same tools and materials as the artist: the same black chalk, and brushes or pens of the same size. If he cannot get hold of the same materials (for instance, a certain shade of faded red chalk) or if there is no need to be so scrupulous (there is very little difference between the line of a goose quill and that of a metal pen, properly handled), the restorer can substitute a more practical modern tool for the ancient instrument, so long as his sole aim is to reproduce the effect of the latter. A touch of watercolour can often replace a pencil or chalk line which has become blurred, and dots of gouache can supply a passable imitation of pastel; they can be used as a substitute in cases where the paper can no longer absorb the original medium.

The extent of the restoration must conform to the general condition of the work.

Restoration is not renovation. The restorer must not try to produce a brand-new version of the original. Signs of wear and age are not an essential part of the picture, but they are testimonies to its authenticity and integrity.

Ill-judged interference by inexperienced restorers or those who are too ready to experiment, or over-persuaded by a pressing client, can destroy the delicate balance of a print or drawing which has never been altered.

The price of such mistakes is the suspicion which inevitably hangs over an outrageously restored work. What is more, over-restoring, like excessive disguising, wears out the paper and accelerates its ageing and ultimate disintegration.

The same principle of discretion should restrain the restorer from filling gaps unless they definitely interfere with the understanding of the drawing, and for which there are some established guides. He must never reconstruct large areas, even if they are a vital missing part of the composition, because if he does, this puts him in competition with the original artist. It would never enter the head of a good restorer to re-draw the missing part of a black chalk drawing or etching which had been cut in half.

Some collectors and curators, while accepting that deteriorating and damaged works should be treated, dislike the restoration of lines and colours on principle.

This respectful restraint may be supported by apparently scientific or philosophical arguments, but surely it is going too far. It is true that the original work of art must be preserved, but always with the proviso that it was designed to be admired. Restoration can make works which have been distorted or injured by time acceptable and pleasing to look at. It is only justified when guided by the principles listed above. This is a matter for the individual conscience.

This is not the place for a detailed description of some of the major restorers' feats, but it might be useful to list some practical aspects.

HARMONIZING THE TONE

However skilfully they are executed, many operations (patching or bleaching isolated stains, for example) leave noticeable traces. These marks often look unpleasant, and they cannot be mistaken for stains and other marks on the drawing since they are always a lighter colour than the rest of the work. Restoring the tone consists of minimizing the difference between the original and the new or treated areas by tinting the latter lightly and uniformly. Liquid, highly dilute tints are used which will sink into the paper without forming an opaque deposit. The most popular are ink or watercolour washes. Dyes and even decoctions of tea or coffee are also frequently used.

The selected tints, preferably of a lighter shade, are applied with a fine brush or an atomizer. Several applications will probably be necessary to 'raise the tone' to that of the adjacent areas. The new tints will become appreciably lighter when they dry; the restorer can then carry out a final retouching, always bearing in mind that it is better to leave slightly paler areas than to darken the whole work.

It is better to tint a patch before applying it; colour

78/79/80
Draft for decorative work. A pen drawing with Indian ink and bistre wash. The gap in the middle of the drawing has been patched after lining the work. The essential lines have been sketched in to preserve the balance of the composition. It is not necessary to complete the washes; a few lines are enough (Anonymous, seventeenth-century Italian school).

98

can then be applied to the whole paper more easily. Retouching *in situ* is usually necessary. It should be carried out with care to avoid any encroaching on the original parts, which can only emphasize the difference in tints. Finally a light dusting or blurring can be carried out with a stump-brush to harmonize the new part with the patina of age.

RESTORING COLOURS

When the tone has been restored, gaps in the work sometimes look less obtrusive, but this work never encroaches on the artist's own strokes. In cases where highly inoffensive correction still leaves unsightly gaps in the composition, the restorer must reconstruct lines and colours, while always strictly respecting the principles set out above.

For colours he must select the original material (gouache, watercolour or washes) unless a substitute seems to produce a better result – e.g. watercolour tint instead of an unobtainable sepia or bistre. Only high-quality materials should be used. It is not enough to obtain an immediate but temporary match; he should be sure that the original and the restored passages will age in the same way. The work is usually executed with a fine brush, which is flexible enough to imitate most techniques. A variety of methods can be used, either a series of dots or a sweeping movement – the important thing is to produce an effect as close as possible not only to the tone but also to the style of the artist. Stippling with the point of the brush is suitable for restoring small surfaces with a lot of shading. In places where the master's hand shows most clearly, gaps should be filled in with a lighter movement after long practice on trial pieces.

RESTORING LINES

Here too it is preferable to use materials and tools (crayon, ink or pastel) similar to those of the original, though some ingenious substitutes are possible. Photographs or tracings made before treatment or, failing these, sketches for the composition, should be transferred to the area to be restored. The lines should first be lightly sketched, thinner and fainter than the original (Figs. 78–80). If the difference is too obvious, the restorer should go over his first line, since he can only obtain by slow degrees what the artist achieved in a single stroke.

There are several chemical processes by means of which faded lines can be reinforced. The latest is an application of gallic acid on lines of ferro-gallic ink (ink of a more or less constant shade of brown). These processes are useful for bringing up manuscript texts, but they are not advisable for works of art, not only because they spoil the modulations of the line, but because their harmful qualities may damage the paper.

When dealing with engravings, it is obvious that, with rare exceptions, no attempt should be made to fill in gaps with the help of a process of identical impression. Reconstruction of lines may often be made easier by the fact that several impressions are pulled at a time and are available for reference. Sometimes it may even be possible to restore a complete engraving from fragments of several irreparably damaged versions, in cases where the salvage of a single engraving justifies the sacrifice of the others. Inspired by this idea, some restorers have gone so far as to fill up gaps in the cuts by matching patches of identical appearance from fragments of engravings.

In most cases, however, line engravings (etchings, engravings, dry point, etc.) can be restored with a pen, and lithographs and aquatints with watercolour, taking the same precautions used for drawings.

In this section the author has set out his own personal ideas, which should not be attributed to the colleagues with whom he often works on these problems.

Mounting and Arrangement

The restorer's job is almost finished. His last duty is to provide guidelines for mounting and arrangement for the framer, collector, dealer or curator. They will not be wasted.

Mounting is the word used to describe the different procedures for holding the sheets of drawing or print in a surround, or grouping them together in a frame; it also includes glazing, boards, bindings and the packing in which they are to be kept or displayed.

All methods of keeping prints and drawings must conform to the following rules:

Hygiene

Materials which will be in contact with the work must be strictly controlled. The mounter must make sure that paper and packing are sterile, stable and as inert as possible; that their pH measurement is not less than 6; and that any colouring matter they contain is fixed and not likely to spread. He should choose hand-made rag paper and wooden packing cases lined with paper on all sides whenever possible. Any other materials he uses such as cloth, leather or wood should meet these specifications. When he has to stick things together, he should confine himself to sizing paste and animal glues, rigidly eschewing plastic tapes and synthetic adhesives or adhesives of unknown composition which will certainly damage the paper as they penetrate it.

Comfort

Thorough knowledge of the expansion properties of cardboards and papers and their resistance to ageing and wear is indispensable to the craftsman commissioned to display a work of graphic art and to keep it in good condition. It must be fixed firmly but without too much tension in a cardboard mount which will set it off and protect it. This balance is obtained by sticking one or more hinges made of mulberry paper between the back of the drawing and the base of the assemblage. The window of the mount should harmonize with the size of the work, and its cardboard should be about 5 mm thick to avoid any friction with the surface of the print or drawing. Sheets mounted in this way may be packed together in boxes or cartons.

The boxes may be stored vertically or horizontally, but it is important to avoid piling them up under pressure. The protection provided by a frame with glass or Perspex for large-sized works shelters them from dust when they are on display. Prints and drawings lying face to face in albums should be separated by sheets of paper laid between them.

Tools used for working cardboard are traditional: rulers, compasses, scribers and set-squares. Cutters and scalpels should be kept very sharp. Mechanical aids such as shears, trimmers and bevelling guides become indispensable as a collection grows larger.

Convenience

Sheets of prints and drawings are rarely the same size. As the collection develops, the need for a system of classification and conservation will become apparent. One of the most useful ways of making a graphic collection easy and adaptable to handle is to standardize sizes.

By adopting two or three sizes of mount, works of a wide variety of sizes can be standardized. These sizes should be determined by the measurements of the works, the capacity of the boxes and cases, and finally the shape of the frames available for temporary exhibitions. Heavy or over-large mounts should be avoided, and corners of the mount may be rounded off to avoid damage in case of knocks. Places where they are stored, such as cupboards, shelves, portfolios, racks, tables and frames should be carefully studied to see that they will make conservation, handling, examination and display of prints and drawings as easy, practicable and safe as possible.

Aesthetics

Taste is an individual matter; but in choosing a mount, an error of taste is an insidious offence against the graphic work. Everything around it either sets it off, or obscures it.

The unobtrusive ivory colour of pasteboard is generally highly satisfactory, but the choice of a mount in a more subtle colour can conform harmoniously with the appearance of the work. A red chalk drawing, for instance, may be pleasantly set off by a blue border, or a bistre wash by a lime-green one.

It has already been stated that old mounts should always be preserved, restored or, in suitable cases, copied – skilfully – down to the last detail of rule and wash, gold band and cartouche. Harmonizing the style of the work with that of the immediate surroundings is always desirable. The work should be studied with care, and respected as far as possible, not only with regard to the mount, frame and binding but also the packing cases, containers and, in a word, everything having to do with the surroundings in which the work is to be kept. Nothing is too good for fine prints and drawings, and this was the spirit in which the great display cabinets were designed.

Security

It has been pointed out by some of the people who have read this text that only the traditional methods have been described – they have certainly proved their worth – and neither miracle procedures nor new treatments have been mentioned. The author's intention was to draw the attention of the collector, who is often so wrapped up in the spiritual content of the work that he does not notice the physical facts, to its fragility and the necessity for taking unsparing pains in caring for it.

The safety of prints and drawings requires constant vigilance, a little imagination and plenty of common sense in looking with an ever-anxious and watchful eye for the imperceptible changes which are taking place in a work of art all the time. Simple precautions and regular maintenance are often enough to ward off irreparable damage.

SOME SPECIAL CASES

This book has been chiefly confined to the restoration of prints and drawings, which represent the majority of our artistic heritage in the graphic arts, but some other works are related to the graphic art by their technique and type of support and can best be restored by a graphic expert.

Pastels

Pastel was first used during the Renaissance (the word is used for both the medium, the tool and the work), and is a drawing executed in coloured chalk. At first only one or two colours were used, but the range soon became more extensive. Modern pastels are still much the same as they always were; sticks 6 to 8 cm long consisting of various pigments and a binding agent, usually gum arabic softened with honey.

The work is executed on slightly rough paper, grey-blue or grey-beige in colour to contrast with the highlights. Other supports are sometimes used, such as prepared paper or canvas (i.e. coated with a layer of chalk mixed with size and sometimes finely powdered pumice), parchment or vellum which appeals to some artists because of its velvety quality as being especially suitable for portraits. Finally, there are a number of special papers and fabrics such as velour paper and the painted canvases on which Manet's pastels were executed, and even panels of roughened metal. The paper is usually supported on a sheet of cardboard or a stretched canvas.

DETERIORATION OF PASTELS AND ITS REMEDIES

The coloured pigments of pastels remain remarkably fresh as time passes. They are, however, extremely fragile; and even when they are fixed, easily damage by friction, damp and knocks. The surface must always be protected by glass.

The Problem of Humidity

Spotting and mildew, encouraged by excess humidity, are especially prevalent in the pastes on the paper and support as well as the binding agent of the pastel. They appear both as dark patches on light passages and as light spots on dark passages, at first forming only a light film but later flourishing luxuriantly. It is not unusual, in extreme cases, to find a whole work completely and thickly covered with mould.

The removal of mildew and film calls for great skill. It is done with a light smoothing movement of a sable brush or a finger tip. Such work must, of course, be executed in gradual steps to avoid blurring the colours, taking great care not to spread any residue of mould. The same process is used for removing dust, aided where necessary with gentle insufflation.

81
Pastel on paper stretched on a canvas backing (Jean Valade, *Portrait of a Man*).

82/83
Pastel on paper stretched on a canvas backing. Badly damaged by damp and extensively torn, it was lined and strengthened, then restored (Louis Vigée, *Portrait of a Man*).

It sometimes happens that there are stains and rings formed by areas of accumulated pastel on the paper which will not take any more retouching. The restorer should begin by trying scraping, if this can be done without damaging the paper. If it loses its facility for holding chalk it must be given a new grain by coating the surface locally with a wash of gouache or a light preparation of pumice.

Tears and Knocks

Creased, folded or torn pastels should be lined with paper and appropriately patched, whether they are executed on paper or parchment. The procedure for lining is the same as for other drawings, with the sole exception of using a fairly thick paste so as to avoid moistening the paper too much and fixing both sides of the pastel thoroughly beforehand.

Pastels should only be treated by immersion in really exceptional cases, and not unless they are thoroughly fixed and drastic restoration, regardless of the risk to their bloom, is essential.

The Framing of Pastels

Until quite recently pastels used to be framed in an unsystematic and defective manner. Sometimes the pastel on its cardboard backing or stretcher was nailed into the grooves of the frame. The overlay separating it from the glass was pasted or nailed to the surface of the pastel. Strips used to be carelessly pasted onto the back or edge of a picture to hold the mounting firmly together – a process which soon proved to be ineffectual, and the backing of wood or cardboard which was meant to protect the pastel was often broken or bent and totally inadequate for its purpose. Obviously there was a need for some systematic procedure.

Once it is removed from its frame and cleared of the superfluous paper, nails, cardboard and wooden boards, a pastel can be restored as nearly as possible to its original condition.

A container is made to the exact measurements of the work. It consists of a frame the same size as the work made of oak, with an L-shaped section. The pastel is placed in this frame lying on the inner angle of the L. The glass rests on the flat outer surface of the L, and is therefore a few millimetres away from the pastel. The mount, which must be a perfect fit, is finished with a backing of cardboard pierced at intervals with ventilation holes. The strips joining the various parts together may be of paper or of fabric.

In this container, which can be fixed into the groove of the frame with metal wedges or clamps, the work will be both free from contact and firmly held in place.

Oval containers can be made in the same way, with strips of cardboard fitted round the curve. This method of framing helps conservation, handling and maintenance. The picture can be moved or put into a different frame without risk since it stays in the same container. On the other hand, it can easily be removed when the glass needs cleaning on both sides.

The process preserves the integrity of the work and allows for the possibility of future alteration or improvement.

Large-sized Works

There are three main categories of large-sized works: cartoons, maps and plans, and posters.

CARTOONS

Paper, which was almost always made in small sheets in its early days, soon came to be used for extremely large works. Etymologically *charta* means paper, and the word 'cartoon' is used for the sheet of paper which acts as a guide to fresco painters, interior decorators, tapestry-makers and architects in their work. The term is applied to works of art that vary greatly in materials, techniques and purposes.

Cartoons usually consist of more or less regularly-shaped paper of indifferent quality. Rag paper was used until the nineteenth century, and then the paper industry began to produce a variety of types such as tracing paper, brown paper and heavy-duty wrapping paper. Techniques and materials proliferated, including charcoal, pencil, ink line, wash and distemper watercolours. True pictures were created – on paper. The sheets were juxtaposed or overlapped and usually backed with one or more layers of paper, often stretched or backed with cardboard, canvas or wood, and finally mounted on a wooden frame or a metal armature. Cartoons often bear the pin-holes through which outlines were transferred to the wall or other surface to be decorated.

MAPS AND PLANS

Maps and plans are often subjected to a lot of careless handling and are sometimes transported over long distances. To stand up to these taxing conditions they are usually made of high-quality, very strong material. Good-quality paper, canvas and silk are used as a support for diagrams and plans, which are drawn with great accuracy in ink or printed and often highlighted with colour.

Whatever they are made of, they must always be lined and re-lined sooner or later to withstand the constant strain to which they are subjected. When the restorer is working on this type of object he must not allow any modification or alteration of the original format to persist. Maps and plans may be kept flat, rolled or folded.

POSTERS

Perhaps the finest destiny for any work of art is to be displayed in broad daylight to the public at large. This applies to posters, but their life-span is correspondingly short. Posters are prints (usually lithographs or off-set) on newsprint, which is one of the most perishable papers. In the harsh conditions to which they are subjected they only survive a few days or, at the most, weeks. Some posters, however, are so beautiful that art-lovers cannot bear to see them destroyed, and magnificent collections of them have been formed.

Posters can only be included in a collection if they have never been used, and even then they need to be systematically backed because of the poor quality of the paper and their size, which can exceed 100 × 150 cm.

RESTORING LARGE-SIZED WORKS

The procedure for restoring large works is very much the same as that for smaller sheets. The most important factor is the execution of the lining for which fabric is generally used. The work is first cut up following the natural edges of the sheets, and then subjected to the usual cleaning processes (disinfection, dry methods of cleaning, washing with water and solvents, removing stains and remains of paper, canvas, cardboard and adhesive tape and, if necessary, re-sizing and treating for acidity).

The new supports may be of good-quality paper or fine linen or cotton or even silk. Synthetic fabrics are only used for paper of no artistic value. The paper or cloth lining, which may be more than two metres square, should be cut a few centimetres larger than the work to be lined, and should be attached to a clean, smooth table or stretched on either a wooden frame without any cross-pieces or an adjustable metal frame, held by nails, thumb tacks or staples. Water-soluble paste should preferably be used. Synthetic or plastic glues and lamination should only be used for objects in current use such as road maps. The paste should be applied to the support with a brush or roller and carefully smoothed.

After the work has been stretched by moistening, it should be transferred with the help of a support (tracing or wax paper) and its back laid on the foundation of pasted paper or cloth. All the parts should be lined up and then, keeping a sheet of transparent paper over the face, it should be smoothed out and flattened, first by hand and then with a paper knife or cold iron. Care must be taken that the fabric does not adhere to the wood underneath it, and it should then be left for several days to dry.

The assemblage should then be removed from the table or frame, and laid flat, rolled or folded (taking care to put 3 mm interstices in each fold) according to the method of conservation chosen.

These processes may sound simple (they are sometimes executed with astonishing dexterity), but there are sometimes complications – the ruinous condition of the work, for instance, or the excessive cost of the undertaking – which defy the skill and ingenuity of the restorer.

Objects Made of Paper

Paper is primarily a flat surface which is admirably suited for the application of lines and colours, but with a little manipulation it can undoubtedly be made to take shape as an object. Creative artists, craftsmen or great masters, have never been unaware of its many possibilities: its flexibility, the play of its colours, its strength and delicacy, its opacity and transparence. They have often fashioned and decorated it to form objects for use, ornamentation or pleasure, some of which are real works of art in shape and construction, uniting design, colour and form. Most of these ingenious articles originate in the Far East.

Ever since the invention of paper the Chinese and Japanese have produced and dispersed throughout the world a vast quantity of paper art, some of which has filled the western art-connoisseur with wonder.

Even a short and necessarily incomplete list of these works suggests something of their exotic and picturesque quality.

They include fans, screens, kites, lanterns, paper butterflies and tigers, masks and quantities of toys and games, dolls and boxes in which paper is combined with equally light and elegant materials such as bamboo, cork, wood, silk, shell, ivory, etc.

Western artists seldom achieve the subtle refinement of Far Eastern work, but for some centuries these have undeniably supplied an inspiration and a model. They originated the Turkish, Chinese and

Japanese styles which played such an important role in European aesthetics.

A few of these objects will be dealt with here, since they can sometimes be genuine works of art, and the restorer cannot help but learn from them, if he studies them closely, a number of techniques which may be extremely useful to him. They provide an opportunity to discover processes which have withstood the test of time and distance, and to perfect but not to replace them.

FANS

These graceful objects for creating a refreshing movement of air are generally made of very fine paper or cloth cut in a semicircle and mounted on strips of wood, tortoise-shell or ivory as a support, hinged together at the lower end. The fan can be spread out or folded in pleats around this point. It is often very richly ornamented with drawing, engraving or watercolours.

Because a fan is made of fragile materials, a very delicate touch must be used when restoring it. The cleaning, re-sizing and retouching is done in stages. Only in extreme cases is the fan completely dismantled, lined or reconstructed.

Most old fans are displayed open, and when they are taken from their frame they lie flat, like prints and drawings. Some of them (there are fans in existence made by such great masters as Hokusai and Degas) have never been mounted.

SCREENS

These consist of a number of frames (two, three or more) covered with paper or cloth and joined together with hinges. They stand vertically, with each leaf (as these frames are called) facing a different way. They are decorated by artists and craftsmen with compositions or ornaments, drawings, engravings or paintings, often on both sides. The supporting framework should be both light and strong, but it can never ensure the safety of the screen. Work which is stretched like this and designed to be constantly moved around is bound to be soiled, torn or knocked about a good deal.

The restorer should try to carry out repairs *in situ*, but he will often have to remove the paper or fabric and treat it like any other drawing, lining it and strengthening it with a tougher material (canvas, lamination, etc.), replacing it if possible on the original frame. Nowadays, if it is valuable, it can be protected by sheets of Perspex (acrylic).

SMALL SCREENS

These are frames covered with paper, cardboard or fabric, sometimes decorated, in a variety of shapes, to give shade in direct heat or sunlight.

The materials are often desiccated or scorched, and must be consolidated by lining or replacing the weakened surface.

DIORAMAS AND PANORAMAS

These small-scale structures use ingenious tricks of illusion and perspective to give the spectator the impression of looking at vast landscapes and lively scenes. The framework is made of flexible but strong materials such as poplar, reeds or cork. The sheets of paper, canvas or cardboard are drawn, or executed in watercolours or gouache in a minute illusionist technique. Human figures appear to stand out in relief. The restorer should strengthen and repair the construction, cleaning and replacing damaged parts. Balsa wood can very advantageously be substituted for the original supports.

TOYS AND GAMES

Ever since its appearance in Europe paper has been used by craftsmen, following Far Eastern models, for a variety of small objects for popular use such as toys, games, dolls, playing cards, woodcut pictures, masks, boxes and cases, which used to be widely retailed by small tradesmen and peddlers.

This is not the place to go into their history, and they would not have been mentioned here at all were it not for the fact that they have a constant charm and interest for creators of graphic art.

TROMPE L'OEIL AND COLLAGES

Some every-day and ephemeral objects have always been admired by artists, many of whom were inspired to select and arrange a number of such objects on a cardboard base, sometimes finished to look like wood or marble, thus creating real works of art.

This also applies to an assortment of real and unusual objects such as cards, vignettes, pages from books or handwritten letters, labels and ribbons, which have all been used to create some amusing still-life compositions known as *trompe l'oeil*. The artists executed these works, which often look deceptively simple, by cutting out and emphasizing each object and adding suitable shadows to give an impression of perspective and chiaroscuro to the composition. These works may be drawn or carried out in watercolours, and are related to the type of paintings also called *trompe l'oeil*, which are done with such skill. They are so perfect an imitation of nature that it is sometimes impossible to tell the difference between the work of art and the real thing. It should be noted that they always depict objects hanging on a wall, never lying on a horizontal surface. This minor art form was very popular in the seventeenth, eighteenth and nineteenth centuries, and in the early twentieth century it had another totally unexpected burst of popularity.

Following in the footsteps of the earlier craftsmen, first the Cubists and then the Surrealists achieved some ambiguous and disturbingly powerful effects. Using all sorts of paper and colours – newspapers, wrapping papers, wallpapers, prints, cut or torn up sheets of music, photographs – great masters such as Ernst, Braque and Picasso transformed the bits and pieces of everyday life into major works of art using the earlier techniques. The restorer should have no favourites, but lavish his care on them all alike.

These types of work tend to disintegrate because of the poor quality of the papers and pastes and their different coefficients of expansion. The restorer should wholly or partially dismantle the work, clean each of the components and replace them as nearly as possible in their original state.

SILHOUETTES AND VOTIVE DECORATIONS

In the mid-eighteenth century Etienne de Silhouette (1709–67) had an idea. He made simple portraits of his sitters by cutting out their profiles in black paper which was then pasted on to a light background. This was the invention of the silhouette. These creations enjoyed immense and lasting popularity. Great artists made silhouettes, not only of human faces but of people on foot or horseback, forming compositions with their scissors which were both large and distinguished. A variation on this technique was to attach the silhouette to a transparent ground, place a light behind it and then throw a shadow on to a wall or screen. These projections were called Chinese shadows, probably as a tribute to their origins.

Votive decorations: Long ago in convents, the nuns' pious hand rolled little strips of paper into spirals and pasted them, piece by piece, into the bottom of boxes, producing an elaborate form of religious art to decorate images and relics.

With the passing of time most of them have decomposed. Silhouettes tend to assume strange grimaces and the votive offerings have crumbled into dust in their boxes. Endless patience is needed to restore them.

MOULDED PAPER AND EMBOSSING

Ever since the first millennium A.D. the Chinese have been making reproductions of engraved stones and bronzes by embossing the relief on to fine-quality, strong, damp paper. Small wood mallets were used to work the paper into every surface, with a soft silk brush for the narrower crevices. If the paper split in the process, it was repaired with another piece. When the subject was completely covered with paper in every detail, it was left to dry.

Then the surface was lightly and evenly rubbed with a silk pad stuffed with cotton and impregnated with red or black powder. The process was completed, and the paper removed from the stone or bronze. It produced a perfect image of the low-relief in white on the coloured ground. The perfection of this method of reproduction has never been surpassed, although it is one of the oldest, and this feeling for the plasticity of paper opened the door to all sorts of moulding processes in subsequent ages.

At present paper is moulded mechanically by passing it between two rollers worked with the same design, one in relief and the other in intaglio, usually heated to make sure that the moulding is permanent. Since the rise of industry, moulded and embossed paper has been used for all sorts of fancy goods (imitation leather, cloth, lace and embroidery), some of which are in lamentably bad taste. Some contemporary artists use this process to produce serious original works deeply moulded in beautiful paper, which show the clarity of the relief when exposed to light. The restorer who is called on to care for moulded paper must confine himself to methods which will not damage the modelling.

It is always sad to leave the fascinating subject of paper, the medium of so many human inventions and thoughts. The best way to finish is, perhaps, with this glimpse of the great artist Matisse. Bedridden, a pair of scissors in his hand, he cut out sprawling shapes from many-coloured paper and arranged them on his sheets to create marvellously expressive images.

GLOSSARY

Acid etching Intaglio engraving process. The metal plate is coated with an acid-resistant ground on which the engraver draws with a pointed tool, exposing the metal. The plate is then immersed in a dilute acid bath, which bites into the lines. The ground is cleaned off and the plate is then ready for printing.

Aquatint Acid-etching process which produces prints resembling line-and-wash drawings.

Bevel Edge of an object cut obliquely. Applies to wood and cardboard, and also to the cutting edge of a metal tool.

Binding agent Used to bind dry materials.

Binding strip A strip of paper for holding a single sheet in a binding. A print or drawing can be inserted in a book by means of a binding strip.

Bistre Slightly reddish-brown colour obtained by boiling soot in vinegar and water. Mixed with a water-diluted gum, it is used for washes.

Black chalk Used since the fifteenth century in Italy. Its use coincided with the appearance of paper and continued until it was superseded in the eighteenth century by synthetic pencils.

Bloom Used to describe the freshness and brilliance of a work in a perfect state of preservation.

Burin Engraving tool. It has a shank of square or diamond-shaped section and a bevelled cutting edge. The handle fits the palm of the hand. Held at various different angles, it is used to cut furrows in the metal plate. Copperplate engravings are made with this tool.

Calender Machine consisting of rollers for polishing, drying and glazing paper.

Cartouche Small ornamental frame often drawn on a mount, on which a coat of arms, a title or some information about the work is inscribed.

Chain line Brass wires set at right angles to the laid wires (q. v.), which they keep in position.

Chamfer   *See* Bevel.

Charcoal   Stick of wood from a tree of the *celas-traceae* family reduced to carbon. Often used for sketching.

Counter-proof   Proof taken by pressing a sheet of paper on a freshly made print or drawing to get an idea of the final effect.

Cut   Incision made by the engraver on a plate of wood, metal or other material.

Dry point   Engraving made with a pointed tool on metal, which is scored in intaglio grooves with rough borders of varying thickness. This gives the prints a uniquely soft and misty character.

Embossing   Imprint on paper or cardboard formed by metal irons decorated in relief or intaglio, usually accompanied by heat.

Frame   Edging of wood or other material which surrounds and protects prints and drawings. The style and decoration of the frame bring out the quality of the graphic work.

Gouache   Water-based colour. It is bound by adding gum arabic, glycerine or honey. Applied to paper, it is thick.

Groove   Slot in the back of the frame around the visible part of the picture to hold the mount and glass in position.

Gum arabic   Sticky substance from some types of African or Australian acacia. Dissolved in water it can be used for pasting or glazing. It tends to flake.

Imprint   Impression in intaglio or relief on paper or cardboard made by pressure or embossing against a hard substance which is also engraved or carved in intaglio or relief. Moisture or heat can be used to soften the substance to be imprinted.

Laid wires   Brass wires, very closely set at right angles to the chain line, which form the metal mould used in paper-making. Marks produced by the wires.

Lithography   Drawing on stone reproduced by pressure. The artist draws with an oily ink or greasy crayon on calcareous stone, and the design is fixed with gum arabic. The printer passes a roller impregnated with greasy ink over the stone. It is only absorbed by the parts the artist has touched. A sheet of paper is then laid on the stone and pressed. Coloured lithographs are produced by printing the same sheet on a number of stones, each bearing a different coloured part of the design.

Maquette   Small-scale model of a work of art.

Monoprint   Unique proof pulled by pressure on a work painted by the artist on a metal plate.

Mount   Container or ornamental mat or plate of cardboard comprising a base to which the print or drawing is fixed and a frame which allows it to be seen while protecting it.

Mounting Assembling and fixing drawings and prints in mounts and frames. The word applies to all the components of the holder of the picture.

Paper-Knife Bone spatula for smoothing and flattening.

Paste Sticky liquid substance spread on an object where something is to be made to adhere. There are several kinds of paste: animal, vegetable and nowadays, synthetic.

Patina Verdigris deposit which forms on bronze. By extension, the greying or yellowing process of paper.

Pounced Drawing Drawing on paper pierced with holes made by a needle, for reproducing the design on a surface underneath it (paper, canvas or a wall), by means of a small bag of coloured pounce.

Print Image impressed by an engraved plate.

Proof Sheet printed by the engraving process. The proof is pulled at different stages, before or with the lettering.

Red chalk Haematite or iron sesquioxide. Known in the ancient world, it has been used in the form of small sticks in the western world ever since the introduction of paper for all kinds of drawings. It was often used in conjunction with other materials such as black chalk or coloured chalk. These three media together can imitate pastels, washes or watercolours. Since the eighteenth century, sticks cut from the natural mineral have been superseded by crayons of reconstituted red chalk. It makes good counter-proofs.

Rule Decorative line of variable thickness drawn or engraved round a print or drawing.

Sepia Scientific name for the cuttlefish. Liquid extracted from this mollusc suitable for washes. Works executed in this medium.

Serigraphy Process of silk screen printing by coating the silk with an ink-resistant substance in places. Laid on the paper, it acts as a stencil, the ink applied with a brush only passing through the uncoated parts.

Size-colouring Water-paint with size added. Work executed in this medium.

Stencil Cut-out sheet of cardboard or metal. Colour is applied with a brush through the holes to form a design.

Stretcher Wooden frame on which canvas or paper is stretched.

Stump-brush Strip of paper or leather rolled up and frayed at the end. Used to rub and blend lines in red chalk, pencil or pastel on paper.

Stylus Now a pointed metal implement. In the ancient world it was used to write on wax tablets and was often made of reed.

Thread-counter (waver's glass) Small lens of great magnifying power mounted on a stand.

Transfer Process of moving a picture impregnated with gum from one support to another.

Vellum Very fine parchment made from calf-skin. Some kinds of paper imitate vellum.

Vignette Small design at the head or foot of a book or chapter, originally representing a vine-cluster.

Wash Process of tinting a drawing with a coloured liquid and its result. Washes of Indian ink, bistre, sepia, indigo and red chalk are used.

Watermark Mark or ornament executed in brass wire on the metal form which contains the paper pulp. This relief design marks the sheet with a visible transparent imprint.

Xylography Wood-block engraving.

TECHNICAL NOTES

These notes are designed to provide the reader with supplementary practical information. They are, however, no substitute for the theoretical material in the preceding pages and the publications mentioned in the bibliography.

Formulae

RE-SIZING

Water:	1 litre
Gelatine:	15 grammes

The gelatine (in sheets or powder) is dissolved in warm water in a double-boiler.

'Glutofix 600'

Water:	95%
'Glutofix':	5%

Synthetic paste in powder form. Mix it with cold water and let it stand one day before using.

ADHESIVE PASTES

Starch paste

Water:	1 litre
Rice starch:	60 grammes

Mix the starch with cold water, bring it to the boil and continue boiling for 5 minutes. Let it cool and remove surface skin before using.

Wheat starch:

Water:	1 litre
Wheat flour:	250 grammes
Formalin:	10 drops

Mix the flour well with cold water, working out all the lumps. Bring it to the boil and continue boiling for 10 minutes, stirring all the time. Add more hot water if necessary. Then add the formalin (a fungicide).

'Cellofas B 3500'

Water:	1 litre
'Cellofas':	24 grammes

A synthetic paste in powder form. Shake while pouring to eliminate lumps. Let it stand for one day before using.

REDUCING ACIDITY

Insoluble ink
 Water: 1 litre
 Calcium hydroxide: 2 grammes

Water-soluble ink
 Methanol: 1 litre
 Barium hydroxide: 2%

BLEACHES

Chloramine-T
 Water: 1 litre
 Chloramine-T: 20 grammes
Rinse in running water; for works which will not stand immersion, use industrial methylated spirit vapour after testing.
Sodium chlorite
 Water: 1 litre
 Sodium chlorite: 20 grammes
 Formaldehyde: 25 ml
Used for immersion and dry bleaching.
Calcium hypochlorite
 Water: 1 litre
 Calcium hypochlorite: 40 grammes
Neutralize with 20 g of sodium thiosulphate to 1 litre of tepid water.

FUMIGATION, DISINFECTING

Thymol crystals in a fumigation chamber
 Ethylene oxide: 10%
 Carbonic anhydride: 90%

This is the most commonly used pesticide. The work must be kept in the gas for several hours inside an airtight container.

FIXATIVE

To protect inks and colours before immersion
 Methanol: 1 litre
 Soluble nylon: 20 grammes
Keep lukewarm in a double-boiler for half an hour, then wait two days till the mixture has the consistency of jelly. It is removable with methanol.

OXIDIZED WHITE LEAD

 Hydrogen peroxide: 1 litre
 Ether: 1 litre

Key ▶
A Print or drawing – front
A' Print or drawing – back
B Base of mount
C Mulberry paper hinges
D Surround, with opening for viewing
E Strip of gummed fabric
F Front of mount
G Spring-and-screw compasses
H Cutting knife with point
I Scalpel
J Square-edge (It is better to provide for the mount being re-opened from left to right, in the opposite direction from a book.)

120

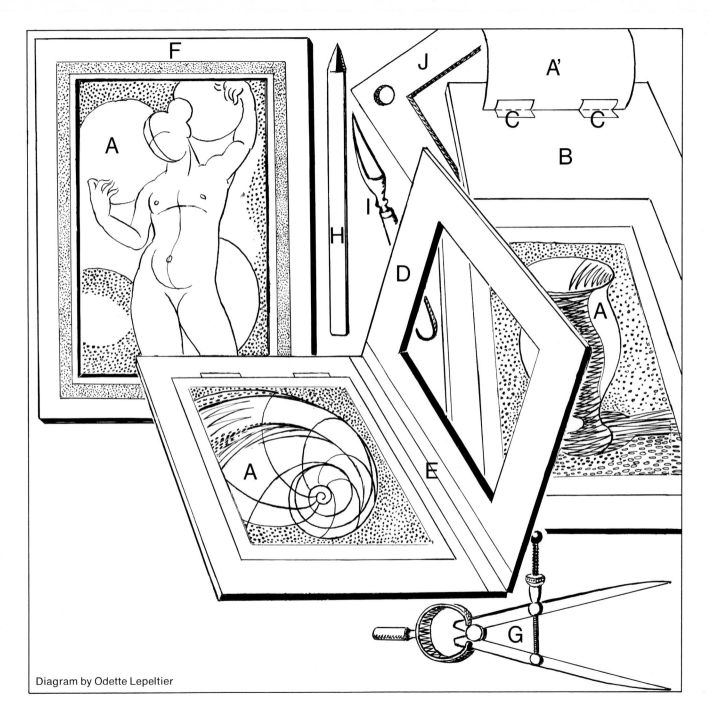

Diagram by Odette Lepeltier

Apply locally, or by vaporization; a small piece of plaster of Paris impregnated with the mixture and placed near the subject will remove oxidation by absorption.

Stain Removers

N.B. Many of these chemicals are dangerous. Be sure to use with adequate ventilation and do not inhale vapour.

STAINS	SOLVENTS
Grease	Pyridine, rinse with water
Oil	Alcohol and benzine
Paint	Hexane, toluene, turpentine, gasoline
Tar	Carbon tetrachloride
Lacquer	
Varnish	Alcohol, acetone, toluene
Gum-lacquer	
Resin	
Adhesive tape	Toluene, benzine, hexane
Wax	Gasoline
Mud	Water, soap, ammonia
Paste	Cold or warm water
Rust	Oxalic acid (NB this is dangerous)
Tea, coffee	Potassium perborate
Ink	Permanganate, oxalic acid, rinse with water

BIBLIOGRAPHY

ADHEMAR, J. *La gravure.* Paris: 1972.

AGRAWAL, O.P. 'Conservation d'objets culturels asiatiques; matériaux et techniques asiatiques: Peintures sur papier.' *Museum,* vol. XXVII, no. 4 (1975): 198–202.

ANANOFF, A. 'Le dessin ancien regardé de près.' *Connaissance des Arts,* no. 161 (July, 1965): 84–91.

Annales du Laboratoire de Recherche des Musées de France. Paris: 1970–.

BAZIN, G. *Le temps des Musées.* Liège: 1967.

BERSIER, J.E. *La gravure – les procédés, l'histoire.* Paris: 1963.

BONNARDOT, A. *Essai sur l'art de restaurer les estampes et les livres.* 2nd ed. reviewed and enlarged. Paris: 1858.

BOUSTEAD, W.M. 'The Surface pH-Measurement and Deacidification of Prints and Drawings in Tropical Climates.' *Studies in Conservation,* vol. 9, no. 2 (May, 1964): 50–58.

BRADLEY, JR., M.C. *The Treatment of Pictures.* Cambridge, Mass.: 1950.

BRIDGMAN, C.F. 'Radiographie de papier.' *Studies in Conservation,* vol. 10, no. 1 (February, 1965): 8–17.

BRIQUET, C.M. *Les filigranes: Dictionnaire historique des marques du papier dès leur apparition vers 1282 jusqu'en 1600.* Paris: 1907.

BROMELLE AND SMITH. *Conservation and Restoration of Pictorial Art.* London-Boston: 1976.

Bulletin de l'Institut Royal du Patrimoine Artistique. Brussels: 1968–.

Bulletin du Laboratoire du Musée du Louvre. Supplement to *La Revue des Arts.* Paris: 1956–68.

CHIAVERINA, J. 'Détermination des charges des papiers – Analyse microscopique et détermination de la composition fibreuse des papiers.' *Colloque International du C.N.R.S.: Techniques de laboratoire dans l'étude des manuscrits.* (September, 1972).

CUNHA, G.D.M. *Conservation of Library Materials: A Manual and Bibliography on the Care, Repair and Restoration of Library Materials.* Metuchen, N.J.: 1967.

DELBOURGO, S. 'Note technique sur la restauration des dessins de Carpeaux.' *Bulletin du Laboratoire du Musée du Louvre,* no. 11 (1966).

DOLOFF, F.W., and PERKINSON, R.L. *How to Care for Works of Art on Paper.* Boston, 1976.

DURAND-GREVILLE, C. *L'encre dans les dessins des vieux maîtres.* Macon: 1902.

EMILE-MÂLE, GILBERTE. *The Restorer's Handbook of Easel Painting.* New York: 1976.

FELLER, R.L. 'Thermochemically Activated Oxidation: Mother Nature's Book Burning.' *PLA Bulletin,* vol. 28, no. 6 (November, 1973): 232–42.

FLIEDER, F. *La conservation des documents graphiques.* Paris: 1969.

GIORGETTI-VICHI, A.M. 'Il Restauro dei giornali alluvionati.' *Colloque International du C.N.R.S.: Techniques de laboratoire dans l'étude des manuscrits,* (September, 1972).

HOURS, MADELEINE. *Conservation and Scientific Analysis of Painting.* New York: 1976.

JOMBERT, C.A. *Méthode pour apprendre le dessin.* Paris: 1784.

KATHPALIA, Y.P. *Conservation and Restoration of Archive Materials: Documentation, Libraries and Archives: Studies and Research.* UNESCO: 1973.

DE KEGHEL, M. *Les produits de blanchiment et les décolorants domestiques et industriels et leurs emplois.* Paris: 1951.

KEMP WEIDNER, M. 'Dégâts et détérioration d'œuvres d'art sur papier.' *Studies in Conservation,* vol. 12, no. 1 (1967): 5–25.

KING, A.; PHELAN, W.; and FALCONER, W.E. 'On the Choice of Paper for Lining Works of Art on Ground Wood-Pulp Supports.' *Studies in Conservation,* vol. 18, no. 4 (1973): 171–74.

LAVALLÉE, P. 'Les procédés et la technique du dessin – les pointes de métal.' *Le Dessin,* (February, 1938): 426–35.

——————— *Les techniques du dessin, leur évolution dans les différentes écoles de l'Europe.* Paris: 1943.

LUGT, F. *Les marques de collections de dessins et d'estampes.* Amsterdam: 1921.

MARTIN, G. *Le papier.* Paris: 1964.

MEDER, J. *Die Handzeichnung: Ihre Technik und Entwicklung.* Vienna: 1923.

Les métiers d'art. (Collection published by Bonvent.) Geneva: 1972.

NARITA, K. 'Le Musée du papier à Tokyo.' *Museum,* vol. X, no. 1 (1957): 21.

Nouvelles de l'estampe. (Publication of the Comité National de la Gravure Française.) Paris: 1963–.

DE PAS, M. 'La composition des encres noires.' *Colloque International du C.N.R.S.: Techniques de laboratoire dans l'étude des manuscrits,* (September, 1972).

PLENDERLEITH, H. J. *La conservation des antiquités et des œuvres d'art.* Paris: 1966.

PORPHYRE, J. A. *Manuel de l'Industrie du papier.* Paris: 1933.

RHEIMS, M. *La vie étrange des objets: Histoire de la curiosité.* Paris: 1959.

ROGER-MARX, C. 'Les dessins à la plume.' *Jardin des Arts,* nº 126 (May, 1965): 32–39.

SANTUCCI, L. 'The Application of Chemical and Physical Methods to Conservation of Archival Materials.' *Recent Advances in Conservation,* (1961): 39–47.

SIMON, H. *Techniques of Drawing.* (1st ed. *Primer of Drawings for Adults.* 1953) New York: 1972.

DE TOLNAY, C. *History and Technique of Old Masters' Drawings: A Handbook.* New York: 1972.

WALKER, R. 'Recent Results of Research of the Barrow Laboratory.' *Colloque International du C.N.R.S.: Techniques de laboratoire dans l'étude des manuscrits,* (September, 1972).

INDEX

The numbers in italics refer to the captions on those pages. An asterisk indicates that the word can be found in the Glossary.

PHOTO CREDITS

The illustrations in this book are from the following sources: Laboratoire de Recherche des Musées Nationaux: 2, 3, 4, 5, 6, 7. Georges Routhier: 15, 16, 19, 20, 24, 25 and from the author.

This book was printed by Imprimerie Hertig + Co. S.A., Bienne, in June, 1977. Photolithographs by Kreienbühl + Co. S.A., Lucerne. Binding by Burkhardt S.A., Zurich. Layout and production: Ronald Sautebin. Editorial: Barbara Perroud-Benson.

Printed in Switzerland